PRAISE FOR CARRIED SAFELY HOME

"I was immediately captivated by this book. Like Kristin Wong, I am a parent to a child, adopted internationally, named Benjamin. And like Benjamin Wong, our Benjamin brought to family and friends a greater, more vivid meaning to life and to the blessings God bestows on us. I fully intend to use *Carried Safely Home* as a resource in my work and know that it will be savored by many as a reflection of their own journeys in faith and adoption.

—Gary N. Gamer
President and CEO
Holt International Children's Services

"Adoption is an often overwhelming and disorienting process. Kristin Swick Wong has perfectly captured this journey, articulating the internal experience so that we don't feel so alone, and then adding thoughtful spiritual reflections that help us to meet God in the midst of our adoptions. Great for adoptive families and for those who draw close to them."

—Jill Barnhart
International Adoption Clinic
University of Alabama at Birmingham

"Here is an excellent case study of one family's experience with two international adoptions—the pain and the reward. Kristin Wong comfortably combines her mother's heart with a delightfully edifying grasp of big picture adoption theology."

—Stephen Board
The Writer's Edge
and former editor *Eternity* Magazine and
InterVarsity's *His* Magazine

Carried Safely
Home

Carried Safely
Home

Kristin Swick Wong

FaithWalk
PUBLISHING
Grand Haven, Michigan

©2005 Kristin Swick Wong
Published by FaithWalk Publishing
Grand Haven, Michigan 49417

Scripture quotations, unless otherwise indicated, are taken from the HOLY BIBLE, NEW INTERNATIONAL VERSION®. NIV®. Copyright ©1973, 1978, 1984 by International Bible Society. Used by permission of Zondervan. All rights re-served.

Scripture quotations marked NASB are taken from the New American Standard Bible®, Copyright ©1960, 1962, 1963, 1968, 1971, 1972, 1973, 1975, 1977, 1995 by The Lockman Foundation. Used by permission.

Scripture quotations marked NRSV are taken from The Holy Bible: New Re-vised Standard Version/Division of Christian Education of the National Council of Churches of Christ in the United States of America. Nashville:Thomas Nelson Publishers, ©1989. Used by permission. All rights reserved.

Lyrics from "Children of the Heavenly Father" by Lina Sandell. Copyright © Board of Publication, Lutheran Church in America. Used by permission of Augsburg Fortess.

Printed in the United States of America
10 09 08 07 06 05   7 6 5 4 3 2 1

                 Library of Congress Cataloging-in-Publication Data

Wong, Kristin Swick.
 Carried safely home : the spiritual legacy of an adoptive family / by Kristin Swick Wong.-- 1st ed.
   p. cm.
 Includes bibliographical references.
 ISBN-13: 978-1-932902-53-2 (pbk. : alk. paper)
 ISBN-10: 1-932902-53-8
 1. Adoption--Religious aspects--Christianity. I. Title.

HV875.26.W66 2005
248.4--dc22

            2005011041

To Benjamin and Josiah

May you be ever strengthened and encouraged
when you remember
that your story blesses others and glorifies God.

You are fearfully and wonderfully made.

Children of the Heavenly Father safely in His bosom gather.
Nestling bird nor star in heaven, such a refuge ever was given.

God His own doth tend and nourish. In His holy courts they flourish.
From all evil things He spares them, in His mighty arms He bears them.

Neither life nor death shall ever from the Lord His children sever;
Unto them His grace He showeth, and their sorrows all He knoweth.

Praise the Lord in joyful numbers, your Protector never slumbers;
At the will of your Defender every foeman must surrender.

Though He giveth or He taketh, God His children ne'er forsaketh;
His the loving purpose solely to preserve them pure and holy.

More secure is no one ever than the loved ones of the Savior;
Not yon star on high abiding nor the bird in homenest hiding.

Lina Sandell

CONTENTS

PART ONE—BENJAMIN'S JOURNEY

INTERLUDE

PART TWO—JOSIAH'S JOURNEY

APPENDIX 1: LIGHT FOR THE JOURNEY

APPENDIX 2: ADOPTION RESOURCES

FOREWORD

In a perfect world, the ministry of adoption would cease to exist. All couples who chose to could bear a child, all people who bore children would be prepared to parent them, and all children would be loved and nurtured by their biological families. Real life doesn't always happen this way.

Just as God redeems our souls through adoption, he frequently redeems each life touched by this extraordinary solution. Individuals and couples blessed to become parents through adoption, birth parents who entrust their child to the care of an adoptive family, and children who need a family can all now experience this gift. God's spirit of redemption marks each situation in a uniquely different way. Like our spiritual redemption, it comes by faith as we walk through our brokenness and grief and learn to accept God's gift.

As an adoption social worker and the mother of three foreign-born daughters (and four birth children), I'm learning what adoption is and what it isn't. It is one way God creates families and allows us to participate with him to pass on a Godly heritage; it is not a cure for infertility. It is challenging, time consuming, and expensive ... so is parenting! It is not easy. It is filled with joy, grown from grief; it is not simply filling empty arms. It is human connectedness at its best and, sometimes, its worst. It is sacrificial, sacred, and profound. It is a journey, not a destination. It is a picture of God's unconditional love and welcome into his forever family. It is a choice.

Each prospective adoptive parent encounters many choices and decisions during the process. At the outset, "what's best for me" frequently articulates the criteria. Good parents, however, learn to make decisions that are in their child's best interest. Somewhere along the journey, we adoptive parents begin this transition. Often times, a child's best interest requires that we choose to "stand in the gap" for their future well-being. We must endure the inevitable delays, learn to give thanks in the disappointments, and choose to think the best of the agencies that assist us. If adoption truly is God's plan, reflecting his heart toward children and redeeming the lives of those involved, why are we surprised when things become difficult? Adoption frequently provides a spiritual battleground for which all parties are generally ill prepared.

Many "how to" books exist to guide us through the legal and procedural aspects of adoption. That's the easy part. For the Christ follower, however, the real challenge becomes the lifelong spiritual journey we embark on when we choose to join God in his redemptive work of adoption. Kristin Wong has captured the spiritual significance of that journey and challenges us to begin the trek. We're not all called to adopt, but we are all called to do something! Scripture teaches that God is a defender and a father to the orphan. He protects their lives. What better way to defend and protect the lives of the fatherless than to become their father (or mother)!

This book is not just another adoption story, or account of coping with adversity, whose outcome lies beyond our control. It's a call to see God in our midst, in our dreams, and in their realization. It's a challenge to participate in God's redemptive plan. It's a tool to spiritually prepare us, not just for the journey, but for the spiritual battle and the incomprehensible task of parenting. In short, it's a great read for those considering adoption.

Every child deserves to grow up in a family … not a perfect one, just a good one. I pray, that God will stir *your* heart to make a difference in the life of a child. May he use this book, to accomplish his will, in and through your life.

God Bless,

Paula Freeman, MSW
Executive Director
Hope's Promise and
Hope's Promise Orphan Ministries

PREFACE

Why put my sons' stories on paper and send them into the world? Current adoption literature advises that adopted children should be the ones to decide when and how they tell their life stories, and though my boys have agreed to let others read about their lives, at the ages of five and seven they cannot understand what it might mean to them later. My children have been entrusted to my care, and I do not decide lightly to put us all in this vulnerable position. So what am I doing?

Our society is undecided and unsettled about the institution of adoption. On one hand, there is more positive press about adoption than ever before. Public figures talk openly and joyfully about their adopted children. More books and resources are available to help everyone in the adoption triad—birth and adoptive parents and adopted children. The number of adoptive families is growing as are their visibility and acceptance in the culture.

On the other hand, many still feel that an adoptive family is tenuous, not quite as strong or stable as a "natural" family. Advances in fertility treatments encourage couples to keep trying to conceive children; adoption is often seen as a last resort. Greater cultural acceptance of both abortion and single parenting has often made adoption feel like the least desirable choice for women in crisis pregnancies.

Into this confusion come the words of pastor, author, and theologian John Piper: "Adoption is one of the most profound realities in the universe."[1] At the core of adoption are loss and new beginning, costly love and redemption. These are also at the heart of the Christian gospel—and at the core of much of our common human experience. Adoption echoes the great refrains of our heritage.

Instead of absorbing the culture's ambivalence and letting it unsettle us, we can look to God to give us understanding about adoption. In the mixed emotions and changing conventions of adoption in this time and place, not much literature has examined the adoption experience through the lens of the Bible. This book can enlighten and enrich both our personal and societal adoption journeys. Its stories, poetry, and instruction have inspired people for thousands of years. God uses this book to speak into our shared human experience, including that which is found in the profound realities of adoption.

The Lord has graciously used the adoption of sons to show me many things. Stumbling through the adoptions with eyes up and Bible in hand, I have learned about God, about myself, my children, this world. I have been changed. I am immensely thankful for the riches that have come with our adoptions. And I feel compelled to share them. I have seen marvelous things on my adoption pilgrimage; it would be a failure of faithfulness to keep them to myself. That is why I take the risk of committing these personal stories to paper.

Gladly, I believe that all my children were chosen before they were born to be together in this family. I believe that we are securely connected to each other. And I believe that God is glorified through my sons' lives. That is robust enough assurance for me to share their stories with others.

ACKNOWLEDGMENTS

Thank you to Dr. Herbert Swick, my father and first writing teacher, whose influence still makes me mark up my drafts beyond recognition.

Thank you to Stephen Board of Writer's Edge and Jason Weber of FamilyLife for their advocacy and good advice.

Thank you to Jill Barnhart, Paula Freeman, Rev. Robert Lynn, Melodie Marske, and Ed Scheuerman for their very helpful comments on the draft. Thanks to the Barnharts for their southern hospitality as I used their home as a writing retreat, and to Tanya Ewing for exerting her creative energy to find just the right title.

Thanks to Ginny McFadden, Jennifer Phipps, Louann Werksma and Dirk Wierenga of FaithWalk Publishing for their warm partnership in bringing this project to fruition.

Thank you to the dear friends at Knox Presbyterian Church in Ann Arbor who have stood with us in worship, waiting, and prayer (and book-writing). Thank you to those in my small but vital prayer team, who spent their valuable time interceding for this book and for the families and children it represents.

To Peter, Janet, Grace, Sarah and Daniel Chen; James, Barb, Abby, Abraham, Paul, and Nicholas Paternoster; and Dominic and Vicky Wong (Yie-Yie and Nai-Nai): I could not have traveled to Vietnam twice, much less written about it, without the countless hours you have spent encouraging me and caring for my children. Thank you. God knows how deeply grateful I am for you.

To Phil, Kathryn, Clara, Benjamin, and Josiah: Thanks for sharing me. I know it was sometimes hard. May God accept your letting me work on this book as a pleasing sacrifice to him. I love you more than … you know what.

> To Him be glory in the church and in Christ Jesus
> throughout all generations,
> for ever and ever! Amen.
>
> Ephesians 3:2

INTRODUCTION

One afternoon while revising this book, I take a break from the computer and sit in a cozy chair, manuscript in hand. Sitting across from me is my 5-year-old son. His bare feet just clear the edge of the chair, jiggling unselfconsciously as he concentrates on his book. I gaze at his beautiful, earnest expression and warm dark eyes, washed in the glow of the winter sun coming through the window. I can hardly take my eyes off him. He is amazing.

Then he looks up. Our eyes meet and we simultaneously break into smiles, delighted to be mother and son, delighted at the love that flows between us.

Later, my little boy is off to play, but he comes over to me occasionally to ask or tell me something. He speaks quietly because he knows I am working. He does not mean to interrupt, really, but he cannot keep from sharing with me his little discoveries. Just like I cannot stop gazing at him when I am supposed to be writing.

A few days later, that same boy lies feverish on the couch. He is whimpering. He seems disoriented, and his eyes don't look right. He cannot seem to answer my questions, and suddenly I am afraid that this is more than a simple cold. Should I take him to the hospital? Has something dreadful just happened to him? It is agonizing.

Ah, the ups and downs of parenthood! Does it matter, at those moments of special smiles or feverish bodies, that this boy came to me by adoption, not birth? Not a bit. I am the mom and he is the son, with all the joys, sorrows, responsibilities, highs, and lows of that relationship.

Some feel that adoptive families are fragile, not quite real. Adoptive families retort that we are not different. Our joys and trials are as authentic as those of any family that is genetically linked. Perhaps we do not want to be different because we do not want adoption to disrupt the flow of our happy, simple family life. We feel entitled to have children, and if our children arrive differently from most, then at least we feel entitled to have other things be the same.

But sometimes things threaten to reveal that we are indeed different. Our children's identities are more complex at the outset than those of biological children. We have given up some control by choosing to raise children whose medical backgrounds do not have continuity with ours (often we do not know a thing about their medical histories). Through adoption, we have added on whole new extended families, our children's birth families. They are connected to us, but exactly how is not always clear. Families that adopt older children or those with special needs open the door to new sets of risks and uncertainties. There is risk of disruption lurking around many corners of our adoptive homes. Adoption takes away some control and replaces it with complexity. And we know that we are different.

Adoption has altered the course of my life. We have not just added a child (and then another one) to our family. We have been changed forever. The adoption stork did not quietly come and go leaving us as we were before. Before we had our sons, my heart did not lurch when I heard about political and religious repression in Vietnam. Before we had our sons, I did not pray so fervently for women that I have never met, the birth mothers of my sons. Certain Bible passages did not resonate to me as they do now.

I cannot go back to where I was before. In most parts of most days, I am like any other mother with her children. But adoption has expanded my relationships and my world. It has changed the shape of my heart, stretching it through vulnerability and difficulty—and also through joy. Adoption has made me uncomfortable. It has made me anxious and sad. But it also has made me overflow with gratitude and love. And it has drawn me near to God.

Adoption offers a rich spiritual legacy. God honors adoption by using it to describe his relationship with us. In adoption, we draw near to the compassion, redemption, and love that have their source in him. Many of us are honored to participate in this legacy: birth families, adoptive families, and the friends who walk with them; adoption professionals, social workers, and advocates. For all of us, adoption, even when it is heart-wrenching, can be a precious part of our pilgrimage towards God. We need not deny the discomfort or disruption it threatens. We need not fear that the changes it brings will destroy us. We can eagerly step into all turns in the journey.

Those of us touched by adoption may miss the truths that soar above us on this journey because we are so mired in paperwork and perplexity, or drained by daily demands. This book is an invitation to look up and see the beauty arching over our adoptions. But perhaps it is also an invitation to discover the jewels under our feet. In John Piper's words, "Raking is easy, but all you get is leaves; digging is hard, but you might find diamonds."[2] May this book help individuals and communities dig and discover the diamonds of adoption together.

PART ONE—BENJAMIN'S JOURNEY

About Benjamin he said:
"Let the beloved of the Lord
rest secure in him,
for he shields him all day long,
and the one the Lord loves
rests between his shoulders."

—Deuteronomy 33:12

ADOPTION AS WORSHIP

Our adoption journey began on another journey. Right after our wedding, Phil and I drove from Michigan to a new home in California. Thousands of miles of driving gave us lots of time to talk; somewhere along the way we first considered adopting a child.

We had recently read *Rich Christians in an Age of Hunger* by Ron Sider, a book that challenges Western Christians to work to lessen the world's disparity of wealth. Sider fills his book with biblical exhortations to provide justice for the poor, such as Psalm 82:3–4: "Defend the cause of the weak and fatherless; maintain the rights of the poor and oppressed. Rescue the weak and needy; deliver them from the hand of the wicked." He suggests practical ways to advocate for the poor. Buried in the middle of one page was the idea to "Have one or two 'homemade' babies and then adopt."[3]

This idea resonated with us. We knew very little about adoption but were drawn to it. The thought sat quietly in our married life, persisting through graduate school, a year in China, a move back to Michigan, and the birth of our two daughters.

Our first motivation to adopt came from thinking about social injustice and was propelled by passages in which the Lord tells his people to care for the poor. We noticed that throughout the Bible orphans are singled out as especially vulnerable, and God often tells his people to care for them. For us, adoption was an act of discipleship, a way to follow the Lord and live under his word. Adopting children is not the only way to keep God's commands to care for orphans and widows and the poor, but it was a way that appealed to us.

After our daughters were born we started thinking about adoption in earnest. I read some books, hoping to find suggestions to help maneuver us through the daunting process. Some authors cautioned that adoption should not be pursued as a means to care for the poor. They told us not to adopt with the motivation of helping others but rather for ourselves, because we really wanted a child: "No one should choose any form of adoption to help save the world. You do it to love a child";[4] and "If you want to do something noble, donate money to a good charity rather than adoption."[5]

Of course we wanted a child, and we believed the child we adopted would bring us great blessing. But we also wanted to deliver a child from a desperate situation. We could not ignore our concern for the needs of orphaned children as we considered adoption. To deny that we were seeking to help a child would be to deny the Lord's prompting in our hearts to provide justice to the poor.

Yet later, when people told us how good it was of us to take impoverished orphans when "you could have had your own," it made me uneasy. Even though our initial motivation to adopt came from God's commands to care for orphans and the poor, pointing this out seemed inappropriate once we had pictures of our sons and especially after they were home when I was a new mother reveling in my wonderful child. Like all children, adopted children bring us joy and deepen our lives in ways we could not have imagined. "This is our son," I thought, "Of course we are doing this. We have to. He is our child."

Mothers and fathers do whatever is needed to help their children because they are parents, not because of general, even godly, benevolence. The adoptions cost us much in time, money, and emotional upheaval, but we did not see those as noble sacrifices. They were what any good parents would instinctively do for their children. The idea that we were doing a good deed in bringing Benjamin home seemed to cheapen the blessing he was to us.

Early on, the advice to not pursue adoption as a way to rescue a child did not ring true to us. We wanted to have a part in freeing a child from poverty. But later in our journey, when we were praised for rescuing a child, it did not seem right, either, because we were so in love with our children that we could not imagine classifying their adoptions as simple acts of altruism.

I tried to sort through the possible motivations to adopt. The warnings not to adopt a child out of a sense of charity are there in part because those who set out to rescue children may have unrealistic expectations about the long-term commitment that comes after the adoption. And they may harbor a patronizing attitude, seeing themselves as heroic rescuers of women and children. Their gaze may become fixed on their own noble actions.

But neither can it be right to adopt only out of a sense of entitlement and a fixation on the desire for a child. There is a danger that parents who think only about their determination to have a child become oblivious to others' need and distress, taking advantage of the tragedies of individuals or countries in order to get what they want. Their gaze may become fixed on their own desires.

Adoption can fill the longings of two groups—adults who want children and children who don't have a family. Should we place the needs of one of these groups higher than the needs of another? In our attempts to understand the motivations for adoption, we can simplify it as just being for the children (altruism) or just for the parents (entitlement). Of course, adoptive relationships are more complex than that. Adoption can be a humble partnership, acknowledging both a distant economic and social plight and a family's desire for a child. The two needs come together under God.

So we adopted children because God commands that we care for the poor. And we adopted children because these two boys were grafted into our hearts, because we loved them and had to pursue them, because our family would not be complete without them. We adopted children to obey the Lord by caring for orphans. And we adopted children because it brings great blessing to our family.

But there is another motivation for adoption that can divert our gaze from ourselves and fix it on God. The Bible links our care for the poor with our worship of him. God insists that those who want to worship him must provide justice for orphans and other vulnerable people. He says that, if his people do not attend to the poor, their worship will be meaningless and even loathsome. Summarizing this, James bluntly states that "religion that God our Father accepts as pure and faultless is this: to look after orphans and widows in their distress and to keep oneself from being polluted by the world" (Jas 1:27). God links our care for orphans with our worship of him.

One of the surprising joys of this journey has been the discovery of how adoption fuels my worship. For in adoption we learn much about God. He himself is an adoptive Father, redeeming his children from desperate circumstances. He sets his love on people who are far from him and creates beauty and love out of brokenness. The Lord commands us to care for orphans because he himself does. He even calls himself their personal defender: "A father to the fatherless, a defender of widows, is God in his holy dwelling" (Ps 68:5). One of the extraordinary qualities of the Bible is what it reveals about the ways God intervenes for people. Throughout the Scriptures we see God entering the world to care for specific people, often the poor. He chooses to enter the stories of kings and nations as well as the dramas of obscure men, women, and children. In Jesus we see God even made into a man who walked on earth, physically touching the lonely, poor, orphaned, and sick. In him, we have the ultimate picture of God entering into the vulnerability and poverty of his people.

God is glorious. He created and sustains the outer reaches of the universe, made hundreds of millions of stars, named each of them, and holds them all in place. He also made and watches each fatherless or motherless child in each hidden corner. He counts the hairs on their heads. He knows the pain of each emotionally distraught man or woman who yearns for a child and each exhausted mother who is parenting without a husband. Psalm 146 depicts this beautifully, calling God "the Maker of heaven and earth, the sea, and everything in them," and also the one who "upholds the cause of the oppressed and gives food to the hungry" (Ps 146:6–7). God, unfathomable in his power and glory, is also caretaker for the weak. He is distinct from and greater than his creation, yet not distant from each small part of it.

God could care for orphans by his unilateral action alone. But he invites us to participate in his work of mercy. Where we do not see justice for the oppressed, food for the hungry, or protection for the vulnerable, there we should go in his name. When we love fatherless children, we are doing the work of God—not only the work that he commands us to do, but the work that he, majestic Creator of the universe, promises to do himself. As we go, we will know him better and be led to deeper worship. Through adoption, we are drawn into awe and love for God. We glimpse reflections of who he is and what he has done, and we marvel and rejoice.

What a wonderful God I follow. He made the universe and he cares about the tears of an orphan. Through adoption, I follow him. Through adoption, I worship.

VULNERABILITIES AWAKENED

Vulnerable—susceptible to physical or emotional injury ... susceptible to attack ... open to censure or criticism ... liable to succumb, as to persuasion or temptation

American Heritage Dictionary

Vulnerability—danger, peril, insecurity, jeopardy, risk, hazard, venture, precariousness, instability, exposure

Roget's Pocket Thesaurus

There is one famous adoption in the Bible. It is a riveting, dramatic story. One evening we took a break from the piles of adoption paperwork and watched Charlton Heston as Moses in *The Ten Commandments*. In one emotional scene, the young Moses rushes from his home in Pharoah's palace to the slums of the Israelites, looking for his birth mother. His adoptive mother, Pharoah's daughter, follows. She pleads with Moses to deny that the Israelite woman is his mother. After all, who had loved and raised him, always giving him everything he needed? Surely his allegiance and love should go to his adoptive mother. Adoptive and birth mothers watch Moses struggle, watch him choose to leave the relationships, culture, and comfort of his adoptive home and return to the Israelites. Moses's emotional encounter with the two women in this film is speculative, but we do know that he turned against his adopted family and culture. His call was to his family of birth.

I watched this scene with discomfort, through the lens of a potential adoptive mother. I knew that the call of Moses was outstanding, unique in all of history; neither the account of Moses in the Bible nor the filmmaker's portrayal of it said anything about adoption in general, yet watching it unsettled me. What if my adopted son decided that he did not belong with me but with his birth mother and birth culture? What would it be like if he left our family and our God? I had been thinking that as an adopted child he would really be my son and I his mother, but the movie stirred up misgivings that by entering adoption I was making my family more fragile. I intended to remember this disturbing scene and not have any of my birth or adopted children watch it, so they would not feel this same turmoil and confusion.

I felt these pangs of trepidation as we began our adoption but was not terribly overwhelmed. Phil and I had thought about adoption early in our marriage, and we both felt comfortable with the idea. We already had two daughters and experience in parenting. We were not emotionally depleted from years of trying to conceive a child. Phil is ethnically Chinese, I am Caucasian, and our daughters are thus biracial. Since we were already a multiracial family, adding a child of a different race was not an obstacle. A year living in China followed by friendships with international students in Michigan gave us cross-cultural experience that we hoped would be helpful in adoption. It seemed that we were in a good position to adopt a child.

We knew that adoptions often involve unforeseen turns in the road, but we were fairly optimistic. Little did we realize where this bumpy, winding journey would bring us. We could not yet imagine the wrenching emotions and faith-testing uncertainties that would come with the waiting, traveling, and parenting ahead of us.

No one told us about the vulnerability. The dictionary and thesaurus describe it well. We felt susceptible to emotional injury and criticism, liable to succumb to anxiety and loss of faith. We were insecure, precarious, unstable, and exposed.

Now as I hear the stories of others' adoptions I see the vulnerability everywhere. Most who have adopted seem to share "the emotionally turbulent voyage that adoption invariably entails," feeling the "grief, insecurity, and identity confusion that are integral components of adoption." Most would agree that "all types of adoptions ... travel a course replete with complexity and intensity."[6]

All parents become vulnerable when they bring children into their lives. Adopting parents add extra layers of uncertainty. We put something very precious to us in the hands of agencies, bureaucrats, and orphanage workers, hoping they really care about us and about the children in their care. We may be misunderstood by both friends and strangers, many of whom see adoption as a second-best way to parent. We realize that our child will have a more complex identity than those who are raised by their birth parents. We worry that there will be adoption-related pain for us and for our child and fear that we will not know how to handle that pain when it comes.

Before the adoptions, our family life seemed to move peacefully. This tranquility was shaken by the adoptions to reveal our weaknesses, our susceptibility to doubt and fear. Some vulnerability was exposed early; more remained dormant until we stumbled across it later in the journey.

Vulnerability first surfaced as we ventured to talk about our fledgling adoption to family and friends. Telling people our plans to adopt a child did not elicit the kinds of unconditionally warm responses I remembered from announcing that I was pregnant. Some people asked if we thought we would be able to love an adopted child as much as our birth children. Weren't we worried about not knowing the baby's background? How did we know if he would bond to us and we to him? Some told us they would not adopt because of the loss of control in raising a child with a troubled past and unknown genetic makeup. Everyone seemed to know disturbing stories about horrendous orphanages and their emotionally and physically wounded children.

I started to recognize the nonconformity of attempting this expensive and unpredictable adoption and I wondered if we were overlooking something important, naively casting our family into unnecessary turmoil. I wished I knew some families who had gone ahead of us, bearing children both by birth and adoption, with happy, stable results. Fortunately, there are many such families, but we did not know them at the time, and I did not have their assurance to buttress my weakness.

As we studied the brochures and applications of several adoption agencies, another vulnerability emerged. Most agencies ask prospective parents to give parameters for the age and medical condition of children they are willing to adopt. Some have detailed lists: premature birth, heart defect, cleft palate, missing limb, blindness, fetal alcohol syndrome, mental retardation.

The burden of checking off this list was heavy. Pregnant mothers and their husbands are not asked to make these decisions. When all is well in a culture, parents hope for a healthy baby but accept and love with the instincts of parenthood whatever little person is born to them.

Choices not available to pregnant mothers were now set in front of me. I hated to deliberately turn down a child with special needs, a precious child created by God who would doubtless bring us all great love and joy. Yet when the choice was offered I did not know what we could responsibly undertake, what was best for our family and the baby. I did not know how to decide.

I started to live with these vulnerabilities, a taste of many more to come. Assurance came when I remembered that it is God who creates families. The Scripture that reads, God sets the lonely in families (Ps 68:6) and he settles a woman in her home as happy mother of children (Ps 113:a) gives biblical backup for my assertion that God creates families. My children—birth and adopted—were chosen from eternity to be alive here and now in this family. If I gave birth to a child with a mental or physical disability, I would trust that she was the right child for our family and we the right family for her. If he has so carefully chosen our children by birth, he must do the same for our children by adoption. God has chosen the child who will come to us. This knowledge helped me when people questioned us about whether we thought we could love an adopted child, and it helped me as I shakily filled out applications. I checked off the boxes thinking of God's hand over mine.

We chose an adoption agency during this sensitive time. We were drawn to Hope's Promise because of their Christian foundation and their holistic approach—not only putting children into families, but also caring for birth families and orphans left behind. We decided to adopt a child from the impoverished country of Vietnam and began to dig into the piles of paperwork, spending many evenings at the kitchen table writing about our childhoods, marriage, neighborhood, and finances. We ordered copies of our birth and marriage certificates. We went to the doctor for physicals and got proof of our clean records at the police station.

We started thinking about the new little person God might add to our family. Friends prayed with us for our unknown child and for the physical, emotional, and spiritual health of his or her birth parents in Vietnam. We wondered about the personal trauma, perhaps happening right then, that would later bring a child into our family.

One Saturday morning we drove to Detroit to visit the Immigration and Naturalization Service office and press our fingerprints onto a computer screen for FBI clearance to adopt. Just as I put my thumb onto the monitor, I wondered about our baby. Was she born yet? What was he doing right now, as I watched a computer screen memorize the lines in my thumb? Other times in the "adoption pregnancy"—driving to the copy shop, dropping important papers into overnight mail, walking into a building at the capital to have the official state seal put on our papers—I would think with hope about that little person, wondering what was happening right then to this someone whose life would soon be intimately connected with mine.

While wondering about this child, I thought about a movie. Not *The Ten Commandments,* not any particular movie, but a story of the genre in which two sets of characters live their lives separately. The audience watches the two plots develop in parallel, slowly ripening until the characters are brought together at the perfect moment, to have their lives evermore intertwined. The Lord is the director of this film, keeping our child and us in separate worlds while he plans for the perfect meeting. He is active on both sides of the globe. Though there may be twists in the plot that make me nervous, the end has already been planned. Confident of this, I am free to enjoy the drama.

"I waited patiently for the Lord; he turned to me and heard my cry. He lifted me out of the slimy pit, out of the mud and mire; he set my feet on a rock and gave me a firm place to stand" (Ps 40:1–2).

The vulnerabilities in adoption can make us feel like we are sinking in a pit of mud and mire. But if I put out my arms to the Lord when my heart is sinking, he will pull me out of the muck and put me back on solid rock.

BORN OF GOD

I could not have expected these two particular magical children. I could not have predicted the ways in which they would crawl inside my heart and wrap themselves around my soul ... And I could not have anticipated that this family formed across the continents would seem so clearly the family that was meant to be, that these children thrown together with me and with each other, with no blod ties linking us together or to a common history, would seem so clearly the children meant for me.

Elizabeth Bartholet
Family Bonds: Adoption Infertility,
and the New World of Child Production
Beacon Press, 1993, p. xvii–xix

My 5-year-old Kathryn has lined up her dolls and stuffed animals on a blanket. At her side are a stack of scrap paper, several rubber stamps, and an inkpad. She takes care of the animals and dolls while stamping the papers. After I watch for several minutes, I ask her what she is doing. She informs me that the blanket is an orphanage and she is helping the babies to get adopted. I smile. I have known little girls to slip dolls into their shirts, emulating their pregnant mothers. My little girl is making orphanages. Never have any of my children questioned the naturalness of adoption. It is what they have grown up with, and it is normal.

But for many adults, adoption still seems a weak way of building a family. Surveys report that many think of adoption as the second-best way to have children, with resulting relationships that must be fragile—better than being childless, perhaps, but not as good as having birth children. Adoptive families cry out against these perceptions. They claim a strong and genuine bond with their children. They point out ways that their adoptive children are just right for them—even with uncanny similarities in physical mannerisms or temperament. Parents try to articulate their deep love and attachment for their adopted children and emphasize the authenticity of their relationships.

A Chinese proverb tells of a red thread that connects lovers who belong together even when they are physically apart. In *The Lost Daughters of China*, Karin Evans uses this as a picture for adoptive families.[7] Adoptive parents often feel a sense of destiny in the strength of conviction that this child is theirs. Some without religious faith still feel a need to explain the miracle of matchmaking that brings them together with their children. It seems that something must have orchestrated this union of people, so obviously are they meant to be together. Some of us have the deepened joy of knowing the God who we believe has so perfectly matched us with our children.

Throughout history there have been many kinds of adoption. People do not always try to make adoptive relationships look like those of biology. But for the majority of adoptive families in the western world, the parent-child bond is felt as strongly in adoptive as it is in traditional families.

How is it that adults and children feel so strongly joined without a genetic connection? What is the role of genes and environment—nature and nurture—in adopted children? Their genes, which they did not receive from us, will mark their lives. Their early childhood traumas may affect them. The way we raise them will also shape them. We hope to recognize the genetic propensities of our adopted children and shape them for good. But there is something beyond genes or environment that makes them who they are, other elements that go into their identity. Adopted children are ours by God's plan, by his work and our participation in that work, by prayer and papers, by the physical and the spiritual. Through all of these, they mysteriously but surely become our children.

The Lord also claims children for himself; his children, too, are made with elements beyond genes or environment. According to the Bible, we are all created by God but are not all his children. Part of the New Testament revelation is of God's new family, made possible by the work of Jesus. God adopts his children at great cost, then makes them his own by faith, promise, and the Spirit.

We are God's children by faith: "Yet to all who received him, to those who believed in his name, he gave the right to become children of God—children born not of natural descent, nor of human decision or a husband's will, but born of God" (Jn 1:11–12). Childless upperclass Romans would sometimes adopt sons to train as heirs and bearers of the family name. The "right to become children of God" in John is the language used in these legal, adoptive transactions. We do not become God's children by biology, but we can indeed be "born of God" into his family. The way to become God's child is by faith: Those who believe in his name become his adopted children. Adoptive families know something about the need for faith, as we stake so much on the belief that we will love for our whole lives someone who is not biologically related to us.

We are also God's children by promise: "For not all who are descended from Israel are Israel. Nor because they are his descendants are they all Abraham's children. On the contrary, 'It is through Isaac that your offspring will be reckoned.' In other words, it is not the natural children who are God's children, but it is the children of the promise who are regarded as Abraham's offspring" (Rom 9:6–8). The Israelites thought they were God's children automatically because of their biological lineage. Paul says that God's children aren't made by the blood of their birth but through the promises of God. He reminds us that God's covenant was crucial from the beginning—a fulfilled promise to Abraham started the people of Israel. God the Father initiates and makes promises to his adopted children; this is part of what makes them his. We, too, initiate and make promises to our adopted children. We sign papers, pledging to take all the rights and responsibilities of parents on their behalf. We commit our lives to them with public and private promises.

And we are connected to God by the Spirit of sonship: "For you did not receive a spirit that makes you a slave again to fear, but you received the Spirit of sonship. And by Him we cry, 'Abba, Father' ... The Spirit himself testifies with our spirit that we are God's children" (Rom 8:15–16). The Spirit writes on our hearts our identity as God's children. He makes God's adopted children understand "with increasing clarity the meaning of their filial relationship with God in Christ, and to lead them into an ever deeper response to God in this relationship."[8] And so we trust our adopted children will know deep in their hearts that they belong to us in a supernatural way that goes beyond genes or environment.

We should not forget that we are brought into God's family at great cost. The faith and promises and spirit of sonship can all be realized because, to secure our adoption, Jesus was willing to humble himself, become human and impoverished, and experience scorn, isolation, pain, and execution. Adoption comes with a cost.

God honors adoption in using it as a picture to describe our relationship to him. He does use biology in the creation of children but adds other elements: faith, promise, and the spirit of sonship. To build families he uses the physical world, but he also adds the mysterious and supernatural.

The Lord of the universe adopts his children. It is a great privilege to reflect him by participating in adoption. We embrace children who did not come from our bodies, and the grace of God adds the spiritual components that make those children ours.

God claims his children by taking those who are far away from him, making them his own by promise and faith, then giving them the spirit of sonship. As an echo, he allows us, through adoption, to take those far away from us and make them our own children. How exactly it is that I have this deep and sacred connection with my children is a mystery. But I rejoice that I do. When I am asked about which are my "natural" and which my "adopted" children, perhaps I will respond that my children are neither natural nor unnatural. They are supernatural.

A MOTHER'S HEART

Report from the social worker, letters from references, statement from the doctor, papers from the bank: all notarized, certified, translated, and sent to Vietnam.

We have prayed for the baby who will join our family and prayed for the Lord to nourish the body and soul of his or her birth mother. Though our papers in Vietnam specify no gender preference, Kathryn has doggedly asked for a little brother. We are warmed by her great desire for a boy, but tell her that God will give us the baby best for our family. Now it is early spring; the paperwork is finished, and we settle down to wait. Vietnamese authorities need to approve our file before they give permission for our agency's facilitator to recommend a particular boy or girl for us. We will then be told whatever information is known about the child they choose; and, if we decide to proceed, we will submit the last batch of paperwork and prepare to travel to Vietnam to complete the adoption.

The phone call comes on an evening in June. I hear the voice of our agency's director: "I have a referral for you." I ask her to wait while Phil jumps up from playing with the girls and races to another phone. We listen together to the very few facts: a boy, born on February 15 (a birth date later changed), apparently healthy, living in an orphanage, described by the workers as "a funny baby." That is all they know. I quickly count on my fingers. He is four months old. We realize that we have no plan for how to make this decision. Do we call back later after we have had time to talk, or decide on the spot by looking at each other across the two phone lines? It feels frantic, but somehow we answer yes. Hanging up, we go to Kathryn, who can tell something important has happened. When we tell her it's a little boy, she jumps up and down, ecstatic.

They e-mail us a photo of a baby lying splayed on his back in a crib, eyes crinkled and thick, black hair sticking up. That first photo, I have read, is immensely significant to many adoptive parents, binding them to their child. But I spend the week restless and doubtful. What if this really isn't our son? What if we have made a mistake? How do we know, after all, if this is the child for us? Looking at his picture, I wish I felt more maternal attachment. Is he really is the one God has chosen for us? Phil, meanwhile, has already claimed this child as our own and is ready to go to Vietnam.

I call my friend Diane in my confusion. She listens and prays for me. What I remember of that conversation is her prayer that, if this is indeed our child, God would give me a mother's heart for him.

Several days later we drive north for the annual week of family camp on Lake Huron's beautiful Prentiss Bay. It has always been a richly blessed time, where I go expecting to be touched by the Lord. As always, there are wonderful times of worship, conversation around the table, and splashing with the girls in the bay … yet I feel continued unease about the baby. But one morning, as I sit on the beach staring at the water, something settles in my soul. I am at peace. I am ready to go forward and embrace this child, immensely thankful to the Lord for resolving my confusion.

I return home eager to tackle the myriad details required to prepare for a trip to Vietnam and to add this child to our family. We anticipate the trip to be within about two months and have no idea that events in Vietnam are working together so that our case will mysteriously grind to a halt. Our attachment to this baby will grow for months upon months, until people question our wisdom in hanging onto him when it may be impossible for the adoption to be realized.

We choose to name our baby Benjamin (son of my right hand) David (beloved).

I remember Diane's prayer that God would give me a mother's heart for this boy. My attachment to him is part of God's response to her prayer. I recall my initial fear and unsettledness and marvel at the change in my feelings towards this baby. The Lord who made this boy intended for us to love him in heart and deed. When feelings of love were slow in coming, then asked for, he responded by giving an abundance of affection. The Lord's answering of Diane's prayer, for which I am so thankful, brings pain with it. The waiting would have been much easier if I were not so attached. At times some part of me wishes I didn't feel so strongly that he was my son. Yet this mother's heart is clearly God's work and to be received with thanksgiving.

Our feelings of love are dependent on God's work in our hearts. Our heart-bindings come from him. This is true even for those most dear to us. Parents do not always feel instantly and strongly connected to their children—birth or adopted. Our feelings of affection go up and down from day to day. I see my lack of love as I live with those closest to me. Sometimes I am not happy about pulling myself out of bed to answer a call from a small child, or perhaps it is hard to defer cheerfully to my husband when we have different opinions. To continue and persist in love, we need God's love poured into our hearts, over and over each day.

God is the source of love, and his greatest commands are that we love. So we can pray with confidence that, when we ask him for love, he will respond. When we don't have warm feelings of affection, we can ask him for the will to love in deed while we persevere in prayer for the accompanying emotions.

Alongside prayer, our love for others also grows as we think about God's love for us. Our Father, the initiator, started loving us when we were turned against him. Christ loved us to the utmost as he lived and died on our behalf. I need to read and think about this love over and over and let it sink into my heart. The Holy Spirit helps: "God has poured out his love into our hearts by the Holy Spirit, whom he has given us" (Rom 5:5). This verse uses the image of a cloud suddenly bursting onto a parched land. "One of the Holy Spirit's distinctive ministries is to pour God's love into our hearts ... what the Holy Spirit does is to make us deeply and refreshingly aware that God loves us."[9] When we relish God's love for us, the downpour will overflow into love for others. "We love because he first loved us" (1 Jn 3:19).

I thank my friend Diane for praying that I would have a mother's heart for Benjamin. I am encouraged by the fruit of that prayer and decide to ask God more often for a mother's heart for all my children, for a wife's heart for my husband, for Christ's heart for all he puts in my path. When love is lagging, let me go to the source and ask for more. Let me also fix my eyes on Jesus and receive his love so that my heart will be filled to overflowing.

WHERE THERE'S A WILL ...

Benjamin is six months old. He has been in our life through photos and a birth date for two months, and he is being woven into our hearts more tightly each week. At end-of-summer clearance sales, I buy a pile of clothes, size 6-12 month. Then I fill two drawers with baby food. We want to be ready to go when the phone call comes telling us that we can claim our baby.

The girls are becoming attached to their little brother. His photo is framed on the kitchen table, and 2-year-old Clara kisses him and offers him Cheerios and sips from a cup. Four-year-old Kathryn puts him into crayon pictures of the family. In spite of her shyness, she eagerly tells people about him when they ask if she has brothers or sisters.

August comes and goes, and there seems to be no movement on Benjamin's case. Then September, October. We are poised for news. We ask people at our adoption agency what is going on in Vietnam, but they do not know. All the adoption cases in this part of the country seem to be grinding inexplicably to a halt.

We ask what we can do. They tell us to pray. Pray for Benjamin, the government officials, the country of Vietnam. There is nothing else we can do. Often our frustration and tension bubble into the question "What can we do to expedite the process?" We would pay a high cost in time or money to bring him home. We think about writing letters to Vietnamese officials, contacting congressmen, traveling to Vietnam.

But more action on our part would not help our case and might even hurt it. Our agency needs to exercise restraint when working in a culture that values conflict-avoidance. We are told of a recent case in which adoptive parents were in a room with the judge who was reviewing their papers. The judge was seated while the husband and wife stood for a long time, waiting quietly. Finally, one of them, fatigued, leaned back on a rail. The judge, perceiving the action as dissatisfaction, evicted them from the room and made them wait in the hall for two hours. They feared for those long hours that they had lost their child forever by leaning on a rail. No, we cannot do anything but wait and pray.

Through this exasperating impotence, I realize how conditioned we are as middle-class Americans to take action, overcome obstacles, and get what we want. We feel entitled to the fulfillment of our desires. We presume that things should go our way, quickly and smoothly. If that does not happen, we usually think that with enough money or time we can conquer any problem.

The "where there's a will, there's a way" mindset is entrenched in our culture. I see it when I read through *Little House on the Prairie* books with my children. Our pioneer creed insists that we can overcome all obstacles with hard work and perseverance, a mentality that has doubtless generated much invention and wealth. Our language reveals how we cherish control and self-help: We try to "take control" of parts of our lives in which we feel "out of control." People "pull themselves up by their bootstraps." More than once, I have had salesmen at the door tell me that the Bible says "God helps those who help themselves." (It doesn't.)

Our feeling of control vanishes at times, those shattering moments that become markers in our lives. A longed-for pregnancy ends in miscarriage. A loved one is diagnosed with terminal illness. But even then we grasp as much control as possible. We read books, become experts, make sure we obtain the best medical care possible, try alternative therapies, ask lots of questions, and, if not satisfied, find someone else to help us. For every crisis, there are books and websites promising that you can will and work your way out of your problems and into your desires.

Many of us would be frustrated, and likely even appalled, if we lived in close proximity with those from a more fatalistic culture. They meet difficulties differently, sometimes perceiving their hardships as the will of God, which should not be changed by manipulation. We would cry out that they should do something: Work hard, talk to people, rebuild, retry—something, but not just passive acceptance.

The Bible does tell us to work and to persevere—but with effort that is built on a bedrock of reliance of God. Instead our faith is often laid on sands of self-sufficiency. We approach our problems with some prayer, but really we're thinking we can do a lot to fix them ourselves. Now, waiting for Benjamin, our hands are tied. There is nothing we can do, so our faith and hope must be in God alone.

We wring our helpless hands as Benjamin gets older each week. We long to bring him home like nothing we have longed for before. And we cannot make it happen. Money, time, connections are useless. Neither pushiness nor kindness, neither phone calls nor e-mails, neither influential politicians nor the best adoption agencies, nothing but God himself can move this baby from the orphanage in Vietnam to our home in Michigan. His life and ours are in the hands of a cadre of bureaucrats on the other side of the world. Our culturally conditioned expectation of getting our way has been smashed.

So I struggle against my sense of entitlement, my expectation that everything must go my way, my raging disappointment when I cannot do anything more to get what I want. And there may be other battles going on as well. The director of our adoption agency is not flippant when she tells us to

pray. She is earnest and intent, advising me with much seriousness to enlist the prayers of others as we wait for Benjamin.
She has worked in Vietnam and other countries enough to
discern that there are sometimes spiritual battles being waged
under the surface of paperwork and diplomacy, conflicts in-
cited when there is an attempt to move children from orphanages to Christian homes. She recognizes that "our struggle is
not against flesh and blood, but against the rulers, against the
authorities, against the powers of this dark world and against
the spiritual forces of evil in the heavenly realms" (Eph 6:12).
In the military language of that passage, we are to "stand firm,"
wearing the spiritual armor of truth, righteousness, faith, and
prayer. We do not know all that is happening in the hidden
fields of this battle. But whether I am fighting against my own
self-centered presumption or against spiritual forces in Vietnam, I find that standing is hard work, when I want to run in
and *do* something.

But when I try to run, I hit a brick wall. It must be good
for me to see my complete lack of control. Prevented from
doing anything else, I can only try to stand in faith, try to
learn how to "be strong in the Lord and in his mighty power" (Eph 6:10). God is weaning me from dependence on my
manmade tools and training me to use his weapons.

Where there's a will ... we stand and wait.

DOES HE TELL YOU?

"He it must be then,
Who tells you how much you are loved."
Need Source

Benjamin is growing on the other side of the world, unaware of our love. We think with yearning of the milestones cherished by parents—the first heart-melting smile, the accomplishments of first rolling over and sitting up. As days pass, we know we are missing these and wonder how many more will pass without us. Does anyone in the orphanage cheer for him as he grows? Does anyone pick him up when he cries at night? Does anyone hold and talk to and comfort him? Is he well fed and clothed? How we long to be there for him.

It is probably good that we don't yet know that we will also miss Benjamin's first words and steps, that we won't ever know when those happen, if anyone encouraged him, or what those first words were. We will miss the highs and lows of his first year and a half of life.

We take comfort in knowing that God is there with our little baby when we cannot be. Benjamin's heavenly Father watches and enjoys his son's growth even more than we would. And surely he is able, somehow, to deliver the tenderness and care that we yearn to give him. Perhaps in the middle of that orphanage the Lord himself is creatively giving Benjamin the nurture and encouragement that we ache for him to have. My hope spills into a poem, which plays itself again and again in my mind for months, bringing the assurance afresh.

To Benjamin from your Mama
September 1998

You cry out in the dark of the night—
Who soothes and holds and fear allays?
You roll over, reach high, first sit up—
Who claps and kisses and gives you praise?
You venture a smile and a hesitant coo—
Who looks in your eyes,
Smiles to your smiles,
Coos to your coos through long hot days?
Who tells you how much you are loved?

If only you knew...
Nightly prayers from Kathryn for you,
Tender kisses from Clara for you,
A home filled with toys, clothes, and hope brimming over—
Here to be lavished on you.
If only you knew your father, your mother,
Longing to tell you how much you are loved.

But who is your Father?
The Lord is your Father.
Our bright hope is solely to bring you to him.
But not only later, for there he is with you.
He can comfort and hold you through all this long night,
He can watch all the growth of his son with delight,
He can play with you softly, in ways out of sight.
he it must be then,
Who tells you how much you are loved.

In the fullness of time, what rejoicing you'll see
When together we tell you, your Maker and we,
When together we tell you, again and again,
Tell you how much you are loved.

During this wait, I often think of the words of Psalm 139. They offer rich pasture for meditation. In the past, this psalm has made me cherish God's personal, comprehensive care over me. Now it tells me that this same watchful care is also over Benjamin's life. There is great energy, faith, and joy pressed into these words that can be released and multiplied when we read them on behalf of our children and other loved ones.

It is wonderfully assuring to take the time to read these verses from the psalm on behalf of someone dear—son or daughter, mother or father, husband or wife, friend in distress. Or hoped-for child by adoption.

> *O Lord, you have searched me and you know me. You know when I sit and when I rise; you perceive my thoughts from afar.*

God knows us better than we know ourselves. He knows those we love better than we do, too, and what is mysterious, confusing, or vexing to us is not so to him. And right now the Lord, who sees when we sit and rise, watches our Benjamin first use his developing muscles to sit up by himself!

> *You hem me in, behind and before; you have laid your hand upon me.*

Those we love and long to protect are covered by the only one who is really able to keep them safe. We pray that God will put a bubble around Benjamin, protecting his heart and soul while he is without family, so that he will be able to receive our love later. This verse gives me hope that the Lord can indeed answer that prayer.

> *Where can I go from your Spirit? Where can I flee from your*

*presence? If I go up to the heavens, you are there. If I make
my bed in the depths, you are there. If I rise on the wings of
the dawn; if I settle on the far side of the sea, even there your
hand will guide me; your right hand will hold me fast.*

We grieve this separation from our son. Throughout life,
we will sometimes be apart from those we love—husbands on
trips, parents in nursing homes, small children off to school for
the first time, grown children overseas serving in the military
or on the mission field—and then the longer, harder separation of death. This brings anxiety and sadness. But nothing
can separate those we love from God. This idea is gloriously
amplified in Romans, in a verse well worth pondering every
day, a verse that can be read with trumpet fanfare or a sweet,
small voice: "For I am convinced that neither death nor life,
neither angels nor demons, neither the present nor the future,
nor any powers, neither height nor depth, nor anything else
in all creation, will be able to separate us from the love of God
that is in Christ Jesus our Lord." (Rom 8:38–39)

*If I say 'Surely the darkness will hide me and the light
become night around me,' even the darkness will not be dark
to You; the night will shine like the day, for darkness is as
light to you.*

God sees everything. What seems dark to us is not so to
him. We do not know what is happening in Vietnam and why
Benjamin has not been cleared for adoption. But God does.
He sees the events and people around us radically differently
from how we see them. We fear darkness will hurt those we
love. Perhaps it will. But to him, it is not hidden or dark.

*For you created my inmost being; you knit me together in
my mother's womb. I praise you because I am fearfully and
wonderfully made; your works are wonderful, I know that
full well. My frame was not hidden from you when I was
made in the secret place. When I was woven together in the
depths of the earth, your eyes saw my unformed body.*

What joy that Benjamin has been knit together by God!
I have not carried him in my womb; I have not been there
for his beginnings. But God was there, creating him, watching
him. God told Jeremiah: "Before I formed you in the womb I
knew you, before you were born I set you apart; I appointed
you as a prophet to the nations" (Jer 1:5). God carefully craft-
ed David before he was king, Jeremiah before he was prophet,
and Benjamin before he was home with family.

*All the days ordained for me were written in your book before
one of them came to be.*

To us, Benjamin's delay is unexpected and vexing. To God,
it is not a surprise. These days and nights were written in the
Lord's book long before we stumbled across them. The unique
life that God planned for Benjamin has already started.

Surely this psalm could also comfort the heart of Benjamin's birth mother, if she could read it. She could glimpse
God's plan arching above the brokenness and uncertainties of
her life. She could see that there was an eternal purpose for
the baby made inside of her and find comfort in her decision
to protect this carefully created child instead of ending his life
in abortion. Perhaps she will find these verses. If I believe that
God has laid his hand on Benjamin, I can believe that he may
lay his hand on her as well.

What a treasure God has given us in these words and in others that speak his promises to our hearts. God has preserved them through centuries of painstaking human transcription and translation. They have spoken to thousands and thousands of needy men and women since the time they were first written. This psalm has inspired prayer, paintings, and poetry. Now it is here for me, inspiring another poem and moving me from anxiety to hopeful anticipation. For the rest of my life, these words will be a balm to soothe my soul and a light to guide me out of darkness into faith. Thank you, Father.

SHOWERED

The women of my Bible study occasionally plan an evening out. I usually await these nights eagerly, but when one approached near the end of September, I did not feel like going. I was physically fatigued and frail, and also acutely discouraged about the adoption.

I was frustrated and anxious that Benjamin was still in the orphanage and that we did not know if or when he would make it home. I had never experienced these emotions, this kind of vulnerability, this attachment to someone on the other side of the world whom I had never met. At times I knew the warm assurance that came from believing that the Lord was with Benjamin, but those times were like islands in a sea of churning waves; more often I felt adrift and afraid.

Throughout this time of waiting, people would tell me that we should trust the Lord, or that it really wasn't too bad, since Benjamin was still young. That morning, some such advice had discouraged rather than bolstered me. Though the exhortations were well-meaning and contained some truth, those who spoke them could not know what it was like to be separated from a baby without any way to bring him home. I appreciated their concern, but their comments left me feeling lonely.

By the evening of the ladies' outing, I felt like hiding in a hole. I knew that I could not pretend I was fine, yet I did not want to weigh down the whole evening with my despondency. What more was there to talk about, anyway? These friends had already borne this struggle with us for weeks going on months. Though Benjamin's case preoccupied us daily, there was no news to share. With the stinging words from the morning still fresh, I was inclined to stay home, but my husband encouraged me to go, thinking an evening out would be good for me.

I arrived at the home where we had planned to meet, and was greeted with a cake, gifts, and the announcement that this evening was to be a shower for Benjamin. My astonishment flowed into tears.

The six of us prayed together that night. There was prayer for the gridlock in Vietnam to be broken, prayer for Benjamin's protection and salvation, prayer that God would build into him through these months something of eternal value. There was prayer that God would strengthen our faith for the waiting, that mountains would be moved in the Vietnamese bureaucracy and in our hearts. As we prayed, I emerged from my state of retreat. I broke down, discovering how needy and frail in faith I really had become. Love and prayers washed over my weary, discouraged soul. Through the safe haven of compassionate prayer I was able to face my lack of faith. My vulnerability and tears made room for God's grace to pour in. The love and prayers of my sisters brought healing, hope, and faith back to me.

I realized sometime during that night that my desire to withdraw had not been just a desire to remove myself from social life but also from Benjamin. I feared that we had invested too much in this baby when things might go terribly wrong. We had talked about him, shopped for him, and allowed our girls to grow attached to him. I had begun to feel that perhaps we should have not entered so quickly into this long-distance embrace. We were putting ourselves in a terribly vulnerable position by loving him, and I felt an urge now to pull back into a protective shell.

But tonight there were pajamas and toys for Benjamin, and cake, and pictures to show him later—plus prayer upon prayer. This shower cut off my option of defeated withdrawal. Instead, it was a staking out of faith, a commitment to claim Benjamin though we did not know the outcome.

The Lord picked me up from the road I had started on, a road that tried to veer clear of pain, and he put me back on the vulnerable path of loving and wanting Benjamin. Yet I was not traveling alone on this journey, but was held and supported by others.

On the same day, some words left me feeling alone and discouraged, while others filled me with faith and hope. What was the difference? Much was the presence of prayer. Instead of friends telling me how I should trust God, we went to him together. Also, these women knew me well and had listened to my aches and anxieties enough that they could guide me to faith without making me feel isolated and misunderstood.

I am sobered by the potential that my words have for faith-refreshing or faith-depressing. God could have always communicated to us directly and privately, yet he places us in his body and reaches us through each other. He warns us of the power of our words for good or harm: "The tongue has the power of life and death" (Prv 18:21). He tells us to be intent in the care we give to our speech: "Do not let any unwholesome talk come out of your mouths, but only what is helpful for building others up according to their needs, that it may benefit those who listen" (Eph 4:29).

Let me be full of prayer when trying to touch someone else with words. Let my tongue bring hope from God. Let me stand with my friends, holding them up in prayer when they falter, spending time to listen well and go to God on their behalf. "The lips of the righteous nourish many" (Prv 10:21). Lord, I ask for the privilege of speaking words that nourish others as they have nourished me. Amen.

HE IS GOOD

From our adoption agency's newsletter, *The Link*:

November: "*We have four children waiting to come home from Bien Hoa. There have been many delays. Please pray these children will be home for the holidays.*"

December: "*We have been praying diligently that the spirit of oppression that is over this country would be lifted so we can get our waiting children home.*"

January: "*We continue to pray diligently that the spirit of oppression that is over this country would be lifted so we can get our waiting children home.*"

February: "*We continue to pray diligently that the spirit of oppression that is over this country would be lifted so we can get our waiting children home.*"

From my personal journal:

November 3—Finally some news. Benjamin's paperwork (in Vietnam) is final and our application has been submitted. Within 60 days they are supposed to be finished. Some prayers going up that it would be by Christmas.

November 25—Praying for Benjamin. Protect his brain. Prepare us to devote ourselves to him so he can reach full potential of what is in him. Help us prepare in all ways. Protect him, help him thrive, help us trust you. Shepherd his heart even now to walk closely with you.

And please move the people making the decision to bring him home quickly. For your glory. Amen.

November 26—Thanksgiving. And Benjamin's nine-month birthday. We put his picture in the Thanksgiving basket.

Early December—New waves of longing. Benjamin has gotten a couple Christmas presents. Kathryn asked whether we would save them or open them now. 'Oh,' I thought, 'He should be here to open them himself.'
Kathryn prays for him at just about every meal, and at bedtime. She is weary of waiting. Clara just bounces around saying 'May I hold Benjamin when he comes?' *Two sisters and two parents wanting so much to have him home.*

Early February—I pray with great earnestness and hope in you that the facilitator's information was indeed right, that his paperwork would be finished immediately now, that you would move to bring him home. Give him a heart and life set apart for you—full of zeal, love for you and your work, prophet to his generation. A heart secure in your love and ours, sense of being called for a purpose, chosen. And please bring him home soon.

People across the country are praying for the homecoming of children in Vietnamese orphanages, without any tangible evidence of God's answer—the same call to prayer is copied in the newsletter, unchanged, for several months. Vietnamese law states that adoptive families must be cleared to travel within sixty days of approval of their paperwork, but the law is apparently without power. Our agency's facilitator in Vietnam sees positive signs and thinks the delay will end soon; she is wrong. The call to prayer, Vietnamese law, and the facilitator's words give us hope. But all seem to be powerless to deliver results.

From our perspective, the right and good thing for God to do is to bring Benjamin home. We know he is able—the Lord of the universe is not thwarted by an official or two in a sweltering office in Vietnam. We pray over and over for God to move his hand and release Benjamin. What good could there be for him in this extended time at the orphanage, when his family is ready for him here? Other families also wait, eager to embrace other children. Weeks and months pass with children growing up apart from the families who want them. It does not make sense to us. We know that God's ways are not our ways, that somehow this must be best. But will we continue to believe, with all of our hearts, in the goodness of God?

I think about God's goodness. All we know as good originated in him. In the gospels, when a young man calls Jesus "Good Teacher," Jesus answers "Why do you call me good? No one is good—except God alone" (Mk 10:18). Our very concept of goodness comes from who God is and what he has done.

The Psalms often call forth remembrance of God's goodness, sometimes pairing a statement about God's moral perfection with one about his generosity towards his people: *"You are good and what you do is good; teach me your decrees."* (Ps 119:68) In other words, God is good and he does what is good. *"Taste and see that the LORD is good; blessed is the man who takes refuge in him."* (Ps 34:8). Or, God is good and he blesses. *"You are forgiving and good, O Lord, abounding in love to all who call to you* (Ps 86:5). Translation: God is good and he forgives and loves.

Other psalms make radical claims about the extent of God's goodness to his people: *"For the LORD is a sun and shield; the LORD bestows favor and honor; no good thing does he withold from those whose walk is blameless ... The lions may grow weak and hungry, but those who seek the LORD lack no good thing"* (Ps 4:11, 34:10). These are grandiose statements. Anyone with much life experience can think of times in which these blanket declarations about God giving only good to his people seem to clash with real life. We are tested in our belief in God's goodness when he does not deliver an outcome that seems good to us. How, for example, can it be good that Benjamin is trapped in that orphanage?

Throughout the Old Testament, the Israelites are called to remember God's goodness and power in delivering them out of Egypt; that memory serves as proof that he will continue to be good to them. Now the crowning glory of God's goodness to his people has appeared: his eternal, redemptive work of salvation, planned for millennia and then completed, at enormous cost, by Jesus. "What, then, shall we say in response to this? If God is for us, who can be against us? He who did not spare his own Son, but gave him up for us all—how will he not also, along with him, graciously give us all things?" (Rom 8:32). God is not miserly with his children. He already gave us so much in Jesus that we can trust his goodness in all other parts of our lives. Jesus is proof that God will always give us what is good.

Jesus also promises that those who follow him will have troubles and persecution, so good must not always mean deliverance from difficulty. The New Testament claims that trials are not counterindications of God's goodness but a portion of his good gifts. They allow us closer fellowship with Jesus, because they produce godly character in us and because they are "achieving for us an eternal glory that far outweighs them all" (2 Cor 4:17). Paul and James both exhorted their readers to not only accept their sufferings but to rejoice in them because of the good that God would bring from them (Rom 5:3–5, 2 Cor 12:10, Js 5:2–4).

God is working everything together in our lives for our good. He desires to abundantly bless us—on his terms. Only he knows what good means for us. Sometimes he gives us

what we feel is good; sometimes he gives what we instinctively recoil from and withholds what we desperately want.
In both cases, he is creating more good in us and for us than
we can imagine, though his blessings do not always coincide
with what makes us happy. God's good does not always feel
good. In C.S. Lewis's *The Lion, the Witch, and the Wardrobe*, the
nervous Penvensie children ask Mr. Beaver about a creature
they have heard of named Aslan. Hearing that he is a great
lion, Lucy asks "Then he isn't safe?" "Safe?" said Mr. Beaver.
"Don't you hear what Mrs. Beaver tells you? Who said anything about safe? Course he isn't safe. But he's good. He's the
King, I tell you."[10]

We can read the declarations of God's goodness in the
psalms with faith in the unseen: If God is withholding something, it must for my greater good. Because God is good, then
it must be good that Benjamin is in the orphanage now, good
for us and good for him, good for all who are joining us to
pray for him, and good for God's Kingdom. If Benjamin is
never released for adoption, if he spends his whole childhood
and youth in an orphanage and the rest of his life in poverty—then God will still be good, and he will still be doing
what is good.

What if I had no assurance that God existed? What if I
believed he was powerful and capricious but not always good?
People do live without this confidence in God's goodness,
often replacing it with other beliefs to keep afloat in life's
calamities. My life is built on belief in a God who is holy,
powerful, and good—intrinsically good, and good to me. This
confidence is the invisible foundation of my life, not always
noticed, but affecting everything. It is belief built with rea-
soned thought, not just wishful thinking. Christian doctrine
has faced rigorous examination by many great thinkers and
remains standing. Its robustness allows me to rely on God's

goodness when I cannot understand it. When storms rage and I am shaking, this foundation will remain.

Give thanks to the LORD, for he is good; his love endures forever. Let us build our lives on the goodness of God.

BIRTHDAY GIFTS

February 26. Benjamin's first birthday. We had hoped that he would be home by the time he was six months old. We finally admitted to ourselves that he would not be here on his first birthday and wondered whether to mark the day. Should we celebrate his birthday without him, or would it be too strange and melancholy, an unnecessary stirring up of pain?

We decided to go ahead and do something, thinking that later he might appreciate stories and photos of our honoring him with cake and presents. I approached the day with some sadness and apprehension.

It felt odd to plan a birthday while grieving the absence of the intended celebrant. It felt risky, too. We still had no assurance that Benjamin would ever legally be our son but were again choosing to act as if he already was—and bringing our young daughters along with us.

But now, on his birthday, my thinking is starting to change. I am beginning to understand why we need to celebrate this birthday—not only so that later he would know that we did—but simply because of the wonder that God made him. This boy has been knit together in the image of God, and God has given us the privilege of loving him, even if not yet in the way we want. As we decorate a cake and wrap gifts, I start to feel genuinely festive. We will rejoice on Benjamin's birthday because his life is worthy of celebration and because God has chosen him to be joined with us in this odd season of his being our not-yet-adopted son.

Throughout the day we receive unexpected messages and cards from friends, telling us that they are thinking about us and praying. I discern a connection between those prayers and this surprising joy in my heart. It is marvelous that others love this faraway little boy along with us. This outpouring on Benjamin's birthday shows me that he is deeply loved by God as well as by people who have never seen him.

Meanwhile, that little boy on the other side of the world is going through his days without us. He has no idea that he is the recipient of gifts and cards, cake and prayers. We love Benjamin and are committed to him, though he is utterly unaware of it. Our love is not a response to anything he has done and is not supported by any repricocity, not even the pleasure of watching him grow and learn. Newborn babes seem to take more than they give to their parents at times, yet at least they offer a soft bundle to hold and the promise of smiles and coos to come. Benjamin has no natural or physical connection to us. At this time he can offer us nothing. Yet we have set our love on him. We have chosen him, and we will do anything we can to bring him to us. God has poured out love for him into our hearts, and we cannot move away from him.

This must be a faint reflection of the love that God our Father sets on us. God has chosen us and so we are loved, even though we may go through days blindly unaware of that love, as Benjamin is unaware of ours. God loves us because he chooses to love us, not because we have performed in any way to earn his love or because we can give anything back to him. As Benjamin has done nothing to make us love him, so we have done nothing to make God love us. "Our adoption is not based on our being worthy or cute or attractive. It is based on the free and sovereign grace of God planned before the world and bought for us by the blood of Christ."[11] It is the love of God that gives us value, not our value that gives us God's love.

I think of a boy named David, the youngest of eight brothers. While he was out with the sheep, his brothers were being introduced to a prophet who was looking for the future king. This prophet, Samuel, first examined the firstborn, but God told him that that one was not the king. Samuel then looked over each of the other sons and finally asked their father if those were all of them. Jesse admitted there was one more, the baby of the family, out in the fields tending the sheep. They brought David in (perhaps while one of the older, disappointed brothers sat with the sheep), and Samuel anointed him as king of Israel. (1 Sm 16:1—13)

No one guessed that David would be king. God had chosen him before anyone knew it—chosen him to be king, writer of part of our Bible, and ancestor of Jesus. Years later, when David was a famous king, God told him: "I took you from the pasture and from following the flock to be ruler over my people Israel. I have been with you wherever you have gone, and I have cut off all your enemies from before you. Now I will make your name great, like the names of the greatest men of the earth … Your house and your kingdom will endure forever before me; your throne will be established forever" (2 Sm 7:8–9, 16). Perhaps David was developing a relationship with the Lord in those early years of his life, but he could not have fathomed the love and the plans God had for him.

In a way, our boy Benjamin is like the boy David. We love him and plan for him without his knowledge. In a way, all the followers of Jesus are like David and Benjamin. God has initiated everything on our behalf. He has set his love on us and prepared good work for us.

We lose some of the sweetness and blessings of being loved by God when we are not aware of that love. But the love is steadfast whether we apprehend it or not. Awareness of God's love does not affect its objective reality. We long for Benjamin to know our love as we hold him and talk to him and feed him and laugh with him. But even though he does not know us, he is still precious in our eyes. This is what I am celebrating on his birthday.

In our hearts, if not legally, Benjamin is our son and heir. We have provided him with a crib, clothes, and toys (and that baby food, still filling two drawers). He is the beneficiary of our prayers, the fruit of which includes spiritual blessing that Benjamin is receiving now, though we do not see it.

Our gifts to Benjamin are another dim but beautiful reflection of the visible and invisible gifts that God gives his adopted children.

In the first chapter of Ephesians, Paul writes a lush, overflowing exaltation of those gifts. He worships God for choosing to adopt his people, amazed that from before the foundation of the world, he planned to make us his children: "In love he predestined us to be adopted as his sons through Jesus Christ, in accordance with his pleasure and will" (Eph 1:5). Paul packs into a few verses an exuberant, astonishing recounting of the blessings that come with our redemption and adoption. God has given us every spiritual blessing in Christ. He chose us before the creation of the world to be holy and blameless in his sight. He has redeemed us, forgiven us, and lavished us with grace. As God's child, I have been showered with gifts. I may not be aware of them all, as I am not constantly aware of God's love. I do not see all of the gifts, but I know they are vast and glorious; and they are my inheritance as God's daughter.

There is a cost to adopting children. Jesus paid an enormous price—more than we can comprehend—in absorbing our sin so that we could be redeemed and adopted. Our family's payment of money and time and waiting and heartache is pale in comparison. But in that pale glimmer we have a glimpse of God's devotion. Through Benjamin we taste a bit of what it means that our Father has set his determined love on us.

This birthday is a gift of grace to me in a difficult season. I sense my heart softening for something new God wants to grow in it.

YET I WILL REJOICE

That is why waiting does not diminish us, any more than waiting diminishes a pregnant mother. We are enlarged in the waiting. We, of course, don't see what is enlarging us. But the longer we wait, the larger we become, and the more joyful our expectancy.

—Romans 8:24–25, *The Message*

I feel like a river, actually more like a small stream, still narrow and shallow. The wait for Benjamin digs my bed deeper and wider. It is painful and exhausting, this fight against anxiety and setbacks, this continual need to ask the Lord to give me faith. But in the end, I will hold more water. This trial digs down into my heart and routs out whatever keeps Christ from flowing freely.

Meanwhile, our agency's newsletter has gladly moved from "Please pray that the spirit of oppression that is over this country would be lifted" to "Praise God from whom all blessings flow!" Something in the invisible gridlock has given way. Ten waiting families have succeeded in bringing their children home in the past two months. Only four, including us, still wait.

On the afternoon of April 22, I talk to Paula, the director of our adoption agency. She says that she has been needing to talk to me, and then tells of new complications affecting our case. As she and her staff have been advocating for us and for Benjamin, things have been falling down around them. It seems there are problems on several different fronts at once.

One of the more dramatic setbacks is a tragedy in which a boy from Benjamin's orphanage died shortly after coming to his adoptive family. He was a favorite at the orphanage, and they may react to news of his death by halting all adoptions. At the least they will probably put the brakes on pending cases.

It seems that things are spiraling terribly out of control. After months of inexplicable quietness in our adoption, there is now calamity after calamity. No one in Vietnam will explain what is happening, and no one can know whether Benjamin's case will be resolved soon, go on for years, or fail completely. It is possible that this waiting could go on and on and end with no Benjamin.

My heart sinks.

Paula continues, telling us that adoptions through their other orphanages in Vietnam are going much better. It would be perfectly understandable if we chose to start with another child. There are many orphans in Vietnam. We were expecting an infant, not an older child. This may not be what we are called to, and we need not feel ashamed if we decide that we cannot continue to put our family through this excruciating waiting. But of course they will continue to work with us on Benjamin's behalf if we choose to persist with him. We should decide and let them know.

I hang up in tears. I do not want to break this news to Phil while he is at work or tell him with Kathryn and Clara listening, and I don't know that I can wait until they go to bed. So I drop off the girls with friends and go to meet Phil as he leaves the office. I tell him the list of new setbacks, ambiguities, and crises as we sit at our favorite coffee shop, picking at the sandwiches I packed.

Together we face the prospect of waiting much longer than we had ever imagined, the possibility of bringing home not a baby, nor a toddler, but an older child, with all the additional complexities that might include. Could we do this? We consider what would happen if the door was slammed shut on

Benjamin, if we were strung along for more months or years before being told it would never be possible for us to have him. Could we withstand that? Could our girls? Should we consider relinquishing our petition for Benjamin and starting over with another child?

It does not take much deliberation. In our hearts, Benjamin is our son. We cannot abandon him, however logical it might seem and however unlikely the possibility of a final adoption. It is not that we feel noble or strong. We really do not know how we would handle additional waiting or a final rejection. But until Vietnam gives us a final no or these ties in our hearts are loosed we cannot leave him.

The next day we try to cheerfully celebrate Kathryn's fifth birthday. My friend Janet comes, bringing a square of cross-stitch she created for us. God sustains me through each one of its words for weeks to come, as I pray for this overflowing hope:

> *May the God of hope*
> *fill you with all joy and peace*
> *as you trust in Him,*
> *so that you may overflow with hope*
> *by the power of the Holy Spirit.*
> —Romans 15:13

A few weeks into the newly complicated wait, it is Psalm 27 to which I cling, especially the last verses:

> *I am still confident of this: I will see the goodness of the Lord*
> *in the land of the living. Wait for the Lord;*
> *be strong, and take heart, and wait for the Lor.d*

It is good to have verses to hold onto and heroes to emulate. I am growing very fond of people whose struggles for faith have been recorded in the Scriptures.

There is Peter, for one. When Jesus spoke some difficult words to the crowds following him, many left. Jesus asked his twelve closest companions if they wanted to leave, too. Peter answered him "Lord, to whom shall we go? You have the words of eternal life. We believe and know that you are the Holy One of God" (Jn 6:66–69). Peter did not deny the discomfort of following Jesus. But he admitted he had no other choice. He recognized that Jesus was the only one who could give him life. His confession is mine: I have to stay with Jesus even when I cannot understand what he is doing. Where else would I go?

And there is the unnamed father whose son was tormented by demons. He asked Jesus to do something, if he could. "'If you can?' said Jesus. 'Everything is possible for him who believes.'" Immediately the boy's father exclaimed, "'I do believe; help me overcome my unbelief!'" (Mk 9:21–24) This distressed man acknowledged that he did not have faith, but he desperately wanted it. His appeal, so earnest and honest, "I do believe, help me stop not believing," is my cry as well. I cannot bring Benjamin home, any more than the disciples or the boy's father could cast out the demons from the boy. But still I know to go to Jesus, who can override my weak faith. Even when I don't believe, I believe.

There is also the prophet Habakkuk. First he was heavy-hearted because of the sin and injustice among his own people, and then he was dismayed to learn from God that those people would indeed be brought to justice—but at the hands of a cruel, pagan nation. He managed to affirm, surely after much soul-struggle, that he would worship and be joyful even in the face of horror. "Though the fig tree does not bud and there are no grapes on the vines, though the olive crop fails and the fields produce no food, though there are no sheep in the pen and no cattle in the stalls, yet I will rejoice in the LORD, I will be joyful in God my Savior" (Hb 3:17–18). His poem of surrender is breathtakingly beautiful. I hope to make its sentiments mine.

How grateful I am to have the responses of these men to times of weakness and doubt. Our trial of trying to adopt Benjamin may not be as historically significant or dramatic as what they faced, but it has reached our core and shaken our faith in similar ways.

A year into this wait for Benjamin, someone asked how it would affect us if we did not succeed in bringing him home. Phil told him it would be like a death in the family. We did not know it would be like this; we are walking into new, unsettling experiences month by month. If Benjamin comes home when he is much older, we know our family life may be turned upside down as we deal with the repercussions of his years in an orphanage. We are not sure if we are equipped to handle that.

But I have enough for now, with the testimonies of those who have waited for God through bewildering and painful trials. I am encouraged and challenged to love and trust Jesus no matter the outcome, to run to him even when it feels like I cannot believe. I am glad to follow these men and echo their words.

The Lord digs my riverbed deeper. I am enlarged by my waiting.

WORSHIP TOGETHER

During the first autumn of our wait for Benjamin, the girls and I went for a walk with an acquaintance from church. The girls bounded ahead, jumping on crunchy leaves, while I told Nancy of our anxiety about Benjamin. That evening she wrote to us, encouraging us to keep trusting God. She said, "I am making a commitment to pray every day until I know you are holding him in your arms ... It is a real privilege to join you in this work of intercession." It astonished me that a woman we did not know well was so committed to praying for all of us.

One morning months later, the leader of our mom's weekly fellowship suggested that people lay hands on me to pray for us. Unknown to her, I had been having trouble persevering in hopeful prayer for Benjamin during the past several weeks. Her inspiration gave me an infusion of faith and hope.

Someone in our small-group Bible study leads the children to think about God taking care of baby Moses—and baby Benjamin. Then the adults worship around a theme of spiritual warfare, with a focus on Vietnam. Together we pray for Benjamin, his caretakers, the government officials, the country.

One father tells us that bedtime prayers with his children often turn into prayers for Benjamin and spread out to prayer for other children in the orphanage. A mother tells me that her young daughters have prompted her, for months, to pray again for Benjamin.

Others seem particularly moved to pray for Benjamin as well. Acquaintances approach us at church and ask for an update on the adoption because they want to keep praying. I am so thankful for the community Benjamin will be joining; he is not just coming to our little nuclear family but to a church body already well invested in him.

I remember the story of the Israelites fighting against the Amalakites while Moses watched from the top of a nearby hill. As long as Moses raised his arms, the Israelites continued to win. But when his hands dropped, the Amalakites gained. So Aaron and Hur set Moses on a large stone and held up his arms for him. Whenever I falter in perseverance for Benjamin, people seem to step in and hold up my weak arms so that the battle can continue.

Something that started as one family's relationship with one child has moved beyond us. God is giving love for Benjamin to others. At some point, their prayer and support for our sake become prayer and support for Benjamin and for others across the world. This is not just about adding another child to our family. God is calling others to pray for Benjamin, for other orphans, and for Vietnam. I am humbled to see the Lord moving his people on Benjamin's behalf as I gradually realize that through this adoption I have a part in something bigger.

It is often when we are with our faith family that we hear from the Lord. Through the prayers of Diane and others, Benjamin was knitted into our hearts. Through talking with friends, we wrestle with our questions and doubts. And then there is corporate worship. In church on Sunday mornings, I feel especially vulnerable but also especially receptive to God's challenge and sustenance. Every week it seems that something in the singing, prayers, Bible readings, or sermons reaches the center of my uneasy heart. The Lord tends and teaches me at other times as well, but somehow worship together is especially potent, and I cherish it greatly. I sing—"with my mouth will I make known thy faithfulness to all generations"—and hold onto God's promise of faithfulness to our family and to Benjamin. I listen to a reading: "May the nations be glad and sing for joy, for you rule the peoples justly and guide the nations of the earth. May the peoples praise you, O God; may all the peoples praise you," (Ps 67:4–5) and pray fervently for Vietnam. Or another: "The ransomed of the LORD will return. They will enter Zion with singing; everlasting joy will crown their heads. Gladness and joy will overtake them, and sorrow and sighing will flee away," (Is 35:9–11) which fills me with bittersweet longing to hold onto that glorious hope in the midst of not knowing Benjamin's fate.

In worship I am lifted out of my narrow perspective, out of a tunnel of fear and discouragement, and placed on a hill where I can glimpse the grand vista of God's plan for the whole world. Almost every week I jot in my notebook a word or sentence from the service as reminder of what has touched me, something to ponder and cherish later.

Most families in the throes of adopting and raising young children need and receive support from family and friends. But this is different from social support. Though we do have wonderful friends encouraging and helping us, there is more. We are experiencing the interconnectedness of God's people doing God's work together. According to biblical imagery, it is organic: "Just as each of us has one body with many members, and these members do not all have the same function, so in Christ we who are many form one body, and each member belongs to all the others." (Rom 12:5)

We realize that we are not isolated but interlocked into a larger body. The small part of the body of Christ with wholm we worship is weak and imperfect. We fumble in our attempts to serve God together. But through this weak body, God is doing something beyond us, something we do not yet fully comprehend. At times in our adoption journeys we are confused, weary of praying, tempted to withdraw. The men, women, and children around us hold us up as they listen, talk, pray, and worship alongside us. God enables them to hold us up because of his plan—his plan for Benjamin, for the orphanage, for Vietnam, quite possibly for many others touched by the ripple effect that has started through our trying to bring this child to our family. As we work together, we understand more of what it means to be supernaturally joined. I witness this with wonder, knowing I would not have seen it if everything had gone as we planned.

WHATEVER YOU ASK IN MY NAME

Be joyful in hope,
patient in affliction,
faithful in prayer.

Romans 12:12

Vietnamese law requires that at least one parent travel to Vietnam to adopt a child. We had decided a year ago that Phil and I would go together while friends here cared for our girls. But my health has been shaky this summer, and Phil thinks perhaps I should not go on the trip. If my illness worsened, we might not have access to needed medical care, and he is not sure he can manage to transport a toddler and a sick wife across the world. Not only that, but Peter and Janet Chen, the friends who were planning to care for our girls while we were in Vietnam, will soon be taking their family to a sabbatical in Turkey.

I am deeply disappointed. My heart has longed to go on this trip. If only the adoption had been finished earlier, it could have gone as planned—me healthy, girls to the Chens, Benjamin growing up here instead of in an orphanage. Everything is going wrong.

I thought that I had recently been coping better with the wait, but Phil's worries about my going to Vietnam expose a festering pocket bitterness and resentment towards the Lord.

Mostly I am frustrated and confused about prayer. Should I keep asking for the same things? For more than a year we have been imploring God to work through the officials in Vietnam to release Benjamin. "Please, get them to his papers today and make them motivated to finish them. Please let it be soon." Maybe I should not keep at these specific "please finish it now" requests. How do I keep praying for Benjamin while knowing that God has a plan? Should I pray the same things over and over? Am I perhaps not listening to the Lord, and thus praying for the wrong things? Is that why the prayers are seemingly not being answered? Questions come gushing out of my distraught heart.

We have prayed for a range of concerns, including Benjamin's spiritual life and our growth in faith. We do not expect to see immediate answers for some of these prayers, but I wonder about our specific requests for his homecoming. Maybe I am not praying rightly. Maybe I am not praying with faith.

What should I hope for? Is preparing for the worst when praying for the best doubting God? I still earnestly hope that Benjamin will be able to join our family. With so many indicators that it might not happen, conventional wisdom says to prepare for other outcomes. But can I prepare for another ending and still pray with faith for him to come home? If we end our prayers with "your will be done," is it a mark of faith or a hedging of bets, in case what we've just prayed for doesn't happen?

What about the grand prayer promises of the New Testament? There is at least one sweeping promise about prayer in each of the gospels. I read one in Mark: "I tell you the truth, if anyone says to this mountain, 'Go, throw yourself into the sea,' and does not doubt in his heart but believes that what he says will happen, it will be done for him. Therefore I tell you, whatever you ask for in prayer, believe that you have received it, and it will be yours." (Mk 11:23—24) And another in John: "If you remain in me and my words remain in you, ask whatever you wish, and it will be given you" (Jn 15:7).

What do these mean? Why does Jesus give us these promises? They do have conditions: faith, abiding in him, laying down your life for the kingdom. They should be read in the context of his other teachings on prayer. But even with all the conditions and contexts, it is hard to believe that all those promises mean what they seem to.

I don't want to rationalize away the parts of God's word that are hard to understand. I do believe that God's plan is better than mine; I really don't want him to give me everything I ask for. I wish that instead of "ask whatever you wish and it will be given you," the promise read more like "ask whatever you wish, and I will give you what I know is best."

I am writing a curriculum for kindergarteners in our church. Each week the children will learn about one of God's promises. When it comes to the week of God's promises about prayer, I wonder which one to include. Maybe it should be "whatever you ask for in prayer, believe that you have received it and it will be yours." But children are so earnestly literal—what if they pray, believing, for something that God does not give? Can they understand the conditions of abiding in him, and of praying for kingdom issues and not just their own? I find a safer verse: "Then you will call upon me and come and pray to me, and I will listen to you" (Jer 29:12). I can confidently tell them that God promises to listen to them. But it bothers me to feel I need to pass over the overwhelmingly big promise and use something that sounds more reasonable. Diane, who teaches the mothers, will also spend the year exploring God's promises. I ask her to please teach about the prayer promises, hoping that I can come to understand them better.

My questions are not new, and I know they have answers in books, worked out by people through their own struggles; now I have to work them out fresh for myself. I know some of the answers: Prayer is not just about getting what you want. It's about your relationship with God, about listening to him and letting him direct your prayers and change you in the process. But I want to know something specific: How am I to pray for Benjamin, and how is it that God promises to answer my prayers?

I feel such confusion about how to pray and what the Bible teaches about prayer that I feel paralyzed and remote from the Lord. Over the next month I ask my friends these questions. They listen, but no one can answer them without minimizing the magnitude of what Jesus seems to have said.

Finally I leave my questions unresolved. My way back is not in understanding prayer but in accepting it as an instruction of God to be followed.

Jesus told two parables to help his disciples pray without giving up. The characters in one (Lk 18) are an unjustly treated widow and a callous judge; in the other (Lk 11), there is a man desperate for bread and the reluctant neighbor he drags out of bed. In both, the boldness and perseverance of the requester is given as an example, while God is contrasted with the reluctant giver. People, even if stingy, will eventually respond to persistent petitions. We must go to our Father with our requests, because he is *not* stingy but delights in giving us gifts. He knows what the best gifts are, and he has the power to grant them.

God tells us to persevere in prayer without giving up. Perhaps this is a clue that the other sweeping promises will not always be answered immediately; otherwise there would be no need for perseverance. I know that I have not labored in prayer for Benjamin nearly as long as many people have prayed for their hard situations. My strength is small, faltering like this after only one year.

After a time of doubt and frozen prayers, I emerge. I start praying again, not with great confidence that I know what to ask God, not because I understand the promises about prayer and am claiming them boldly, but simply because he commands persistent prayer. My eyes have been opened to see that I am not good at perseverance without immediate results. But I will try to learn to pray without the understanding I desire. Jesus was gracious to his disciples in teaching them how to pray, and he will be gracious to teach me, too. I do not understand all of his promises, but I have enough to keep going. A weak child, I tentatively cast myself back on my strong Father.

WAITING WELL

Benjamin's case continues to languish. People ask us how long we will wait: When will we move on and start the adoption of a different child? We understand the logic of starting a new adoption, especially since many other orphans in Vietnam need homes. Perhaps this protracted wait is unhealthy for our family. We would not criticize others who chose differently, yet we feel this boy is our son and cannot let go of him until all doors are closed or the Lord releases us from this possessive love.

There is no indication that anything will change. We entreat our adoption agency to suggest something we can do. What about traveling to Vietnam to politely but persistently appeal for Benjamin? No, they answer, that would probably not help our case and might even endanger it. We know they are doing all they can.

We wait. And we continue in our daily lives. Kathryn starts kindergarten; we celebrate Clara's third birthday and the wedding of Phil's brother. Life does not stop, nor does it always feel miserable. But the waiting colors everything. We feel an undercurrent of loss under the flow of daily life because Benjamin is growing up so far away. Often I keep an ear open for the ring of the phone, hoping for good news. Around the activity of life hovers hope for an end to our wait.

Sometimes I wake in the middle of the night and try to calm my unsettled soul with Scripture. For a period of time, the verse I first think of is, "Hope deferred makes the heart sick, but a longing fulfilled is a tree of life" (Prv 13:12). I try to call to mind something more encouraging, but that statement lodges itself in my thoughts. Deferred hope is making my heart sick.

When more awake, I meditate on verses about waiting. "Wait for the LORD; be strong, and take heart, and wait for the LORD" (Ps 27:14). As I wait for Benjamin, the Lord challenges me to wait for him. What does it mean, this phrase "wait for the Lord"? What do *I do* to wait?

Waiting seems important, something God often gives to his people in their pilgrimages. Abraham knew what his happy ending would be: a son, who would have sons and grandsons innumerable for everlasting posterity. His work for many years was to wait for that son. Abraham and Sarah became restless for the promise to be fulfilled. The length of the wait made it seem there must have been a misunderstanding, so Sarah thought of a way to make the promise come true by letting Abraham conceive a child through her servant Hagar. Hagar did bear Abraham's child, but later, when the promised Isaac came, Sarah could not bear the sight of the other boy, beginning generations of hostility between the half-brothers. At times Abraham and Sarah waited well, but their lapse in faithful waiting brought deep and long-lasting pain.

The Bible is full of stories of others who waited. Some show faith in their waiting, and some do not. Some inspire and others warn. The Israelites, desperate for deliverance from slavery in Egypt, called out to the Lord—and waited. Later, miraculously on their way to their promised home, they failed in faith and had to live in the desert for forty more years, passing their wait on to their children.

David was also homeless during his waiting years, running and hiding from Saul. He refused to force God's plan; he would not seize the monarchy when he had the opportunity, even though Samuel had already anointed him as the king of Israel. David chose to wait.

Nehemiah, exiled in Babylon, received distressing news

that the walls of Jerusalem had been destroyed. He longed to rebuild them. As cupbearer to the king, he was in a strategic position to ask for and lead an expedition of his people back to Jerusalem. Yet he also chose to wait, praying and fasting for four months before asking the king to let him go.

The nation of Israel waited together for the Messiah whom their prophets promised would come to save them. Their identity for hundreds of years was that of a people who waited.

Then, in the bridge between the Old and New Testaments, we meet Simeon and Anna. Simeon was a righteous and devout man. The Holy Spirit had promised him that he would not die until he saw Christ. When Mary and Joseph brought 8-day-old Jesus to the temple, Simeon recognized him, took him in his arms, and praised God. How many years had Simeon been waiting from the time of God's promise to its fulfillment? Did he know that he would meet the Messiah as a newborn baby? We do not know. But it seems that he was waiting expectantly and with faith.

Anna appears on the same day. She had been married seven years when her husband died. Had she waited for another husband? Had there not been a brother of her husband to marry her as the law prescribed? Years ago, had she waited in longing for a family? We do not know. But by this time of her life she prayed at the temple night and day. She, too, was surely waiting for the Messiah, a waiting that was fulfilled at the end of her life, when she saw, recognized, and prophesied about him. Simeon and Anna show us faithful waiting, a waiting that does not know the time or means of fulfillment, that worships the Lord while it waits, ever alert for his appearing.

We may enjoy waiting for a short time when fairly sure of a pleasurable outcome. We bear it even when uncomfortable when we know it has a finite end. But we do not like waiting when the length and outcome are unknown. We like to see around the bend in the road, to know what is coming and when. It would be easier to wait, for my single friend who yearns for marriage, if she knew whether or when that was in God's plan for her. The critical illness of a loved one is so agonizing in part because we do not know how it will end. The wait for the return of a rebellious child would be less painful if we were certain that someday he would come back. And waiting to adopt a child is hard when it goes on month after month with outcome unknown.

Perhaps these waits in our life strengthen us for the ultimate wait. For Jesus told us to wait for his return, and gave us parables to show us how to do it well. He said that we are like maids expecting a bridegroom. Some are ready to wait, with extra oil for their lamps. Others run out of oil and then are shut out of the wedding banquet. So "keep watch, because you do not know the day or the hour" (Mt 25:1–13).

Jesus tells us to give attention to how we wait for him.

Abram waited for God's promised son. Anna and Simeon waited for God's promised Messiah. We wait for God's promised return. And also wait for a baby.

The ache and uncertainty of our waiting can sharpen our longing for God to return and make all things new. I do want to wait with faith and dignity, as I imagine Anna and Simeon did, and not like Sarah and Abraham in their caving moment of weakness. I want to worship while waiting. I want to have staying power, not faltering when the wait is long.

Our opportunity for waiting well is now; when Jesus arrives, it will be over. He tells us to think about how we wait, alert for his coming while we worship and work for him. Perhaps we can take these trials as gifts, exercises that teach us how to keep oil in our lamps, so that we do well for the wait that matters most.

TIME TO PACK

On a Thursday in October, the girls and I are eating lunch when the phone rings. It is Jennifer, our social worker from Hope's Promise, who joyfully asks, "Are you ready to pack your bags?" I respond: "You're kidding." Then, my heart suspended: "No, you wouldn't joke about that, would you?" She tells us that we are to be in Vietnam in about three weeks, for an adoption court date of November 8. I fumble around in my surprise groping for assurance that it is really true. I hang up and hug Kathryn, then make a string of phone calls to Phil and others.

The next days are filled with calls. People who have waited with us are excited, sharing our relieved joy and relishing the taste of God's goodness that comes with this answered prayer. Hope's Promise sends flowers with a card: "Congratulations. Praise God. We're so happy for you." Then an e-card arrives from the Chens in Turkey: "Congratulations on your bouncing baby boy!"—complete with animated baby bouncing to a catchy tune.

Oddly, I do not yet feel that joy. For two days I am in a distracted daze, unfocused, unable to settle down to get ready for this journey we have so longed for. I wander back and forth between the flowers and the bouncing baby, staring at them as if to imprint their joyful assurance on my brain. There is so much to do, including deciding whether I should go on the trip. We need to gather clothes and food, acquire visas and airline tickets. Yet it doesn't seem real. Perhaps I am afraid to believe, after having prepared for the trip the other times I thought it was imminent.

I finally feel the impact of the news during worship with our Bible study group on Saturday night. While singing and praying with the friends who have stood with us throughout the wait, it sinks into my heart that Benjamin will be coming home to be with us, and my joy is unbound.

But just before that joy, the initial flush of emotion as I emerge from dazed fogginess is, surprisingly, one of regret at leaving this phase of life. I know that this difficult time has given me opportunity to grow near to the Lord in new ways. I wonder if I learned everything I could. Did I cherish this discipline and not despise it? Will there be lasting effects from this chapter of my life as I move to the next? I do hope I have made the most of the time of waiting, and have changed and grown in faith. All these thoughts wash over me while I sing and pray with friends. I am startled and a bit amused—I was not expecting any feelings of regret at leaving behind this painful time. I wonder if that will be our feeling at the end of life, if we will look back, recognizing the challenging opportunities the Lord provided for us to learn to trust him, and hoping that we did not squander or complain them away.

There are exultant and joyful moments in the next several weeks. I am gleeful when buying applesauce cups, juice boxes, and diapers, telling the cashier all about my boy Benjamin. I rejoice in anticipation of changing those diapers, of finally physically caring for this child as we have longed to. There is a feeling of victory as we anticipate God bringing Benjamin out of an orphanage and into a family.

But it does not take long for me to discover that the opportunities to grow in faith have not evaporated now that our adoption has been approved. Temptations to stress and anxiety come on hard. There is the challenge of talking with Phil about whether I should go with him on the trip; I yearn to go, but he is still concerned about my health. After we have decided that we will both travel, the amount of work looms large—I have to prepare everything for Benjamin as well as for the girls who will stay with the friends who have generously offered to care for them. I toss and turn in bed, thinking through all the details.

A week before we leave I wake up feeling the achy, sniffly start of a cold; I cry out for God to make my body strong. Two days before departure I am overwhelmed with fear of flying, something I have never experienced. I am afraid to leave my small girls and fly to the other side of the world; I wonder whether we should have bought tickets on separate planes, just in case.

And I wonder what Benjamin will be like, what physical and emotional needs he will have coming out of the orphanage—and how it will affect the rest of us. The fears are magnified because they do not affect me alone. In entering this transition, we are ushering the whole family into the unknown.

I need not worry that the opportunities for me to learn to trust the Lord are over with this tremendous development. God has answered our prayer that Benjamin would be released; he worked in the hearts and hands of people in Vietnam to make it happen. He has also answered my heart's prayer that I would have more opportunities to grow in faith, as I find myself tempted, stretched, and vulnerable in many ways.

On the Sunday before we leave, I worship with Kathryn in my arms; I think of being apart from her the next three Sundays, knowing that so much will happen between now and when we return. In worship, I entrust my family to God as best I can. After the service, I slip into a quiet room with my Bible, seeking fresh faith. He blesses me with Psalm 139, that bulwark for times of turmoil. Months ago, the verses at the beginning of the psalm encouraged me to trust in God's watchful care of Benjamin. Now I find the latter verses to steady me.

"How precious to me are your thoughts, O God! How vast is the sum of them! Were I to count them, they would outnumber the grains of sand" (Ps 139:17–18a). Let me be eager to go to you and cherish your thoughts. They are precious and vast, and they will comfort me and give me wisdom, joy, and freedom instead of fear. Let me drink deeply from your word these next weeks.

"When I awake I am still with you" (Ps 139:18b). In these wakeful nights, let me turn to you and be glad to be in your presence. When I am awake, let me bask in the presence of God. Let me turn from restlessness to rest in you. I want to move away from this stressed worry and fear and towards faith. Then I will be able to enjoy all the turns in this story as you unfold it.

I want the abundant life and freedom and joy that you give. I want to fully enjoy this time through deep abiding faith. Help me trust and rest, and give me solid faith so that I can greatly rejoice in this wonderful work you are doing. Amen.

IN OUR ARMS

It is Thursday, November 4, and we are on the plane. Often in the last year, I would gaze at planes overhead, imagining what it would be like to be flying to Vietnam to claim Benjamin. I wondered what praise would be in my heart when the time finally came. Now I am on that plane and have discovered that the praise, though present, needs to share attention with the ache of leaving Kathryn and Clara; an exhausted numbness has also settled on me after the intensity of the last several weeks.

We travel for hours upon hours, through the day and a long, stretched-out night, from Detroit to San Francisco and San Francisco to Hong Kong. Across a continent and across an ocean. As the miles pass under us, I feel as if I am in the middle of a blank page between chapters of my life. The past is finished and the future unknown. Somewhere over the middle of the dark Pacific, I open the window shade and my breath is taken away by the sight of a blanket of thousands of stars that look near enough to touch. We are suspended between earth and space, moving across the ocean with the moon. Two friends gave us cards for traveling encouragement, both with the faith-infused words of Psalm 121. They remind us that God is awake and watchful through this extended night:

> He will not let your foot slip—he who watches over you will not slumber; indeed, he who watches over Israel will neither slumber nor sleep. The Lord watches over you—the Lord is your shade at your right hand;

the sun will not harm you by day, nor the moon by night. The Lord will keep you from all harm—he will watch over your life; the LORD will watch over your coming and going both now and forevermore (Ps 121:3–8).

In Hong Kong, the sun finally catches up with us. We watch it come up over the mountains. We board our last flight, and thirty-three hours after the goodbyes with our girls, we touch down in Ho Chi Minh City, hearts racing. As we exit the plane, a wall of thick, hot air hits us, though it is not yet ten in the morning. We move from checkpoint to checkpoint, overseen by customs officials and young soldiers. Leaving the airport, we move towards a wall of staring people, thankful to find a man holding a sign that says "Philip Wong." He escorts us to the hotel's vintage black Mercedes, into which we stuff our heaps of luggage.

We thoroughly enjoy the sensory feast of a ride through Ho Chi Minh City. The streets are teeming with life. Rivers of bikes, mopeds, and motorcycles glide along, mostly calmly. Sometimes they carry a family, sometimes piles of fresh fruit, or furniture, creatively tied on. Taxis honk their way through the current, and the river of cycles temporarily carves out space just big enough to let them through, then closes back in around them. Out of open streetside shops spill people eating noodles, drinking soda, sitting at low tables, and watching the world go by. It feels so different from a big city in the United States, where people are insulated in private cars, or detached on cell phones—crowded perhaps, but in private worlds. There is a hot and humid vibrancy to all this life mingled on the street. The neighborhoods are not bound by tidy zoning laws. Cramped shops and tall apartment buildings and narrow hotels and outside vendors all jumble together; laundry hangs to dry next to the mango seller, roosters wander outside the noodle shop, and a grandmother squats on a stool on the sidewalk and feeds her grandson.

Through the colorful tumult we reach our destination, a narrow hotel on a narrow street of buildings wedged together. We thank the driver with nods and smiles, wondering if he is amused by Americans and all their baggage. Then we work at communicating the necessary essentials with the hotel's front desk staff. We are glad to arrive at our room, expecting to settle and rest and become a bit acclimated to this environment before meeting Benjamin on Monday. There is a message waiting from Ms. Jan, one of the facilitator's Vietnamese staff. We tinker with the phone until we successfully connect with her.

The conversation goes like this:

Jan: Would you like to go see your son?

Phil: That would be great!

Jan: I'll be there with a driver in twenty minutes.

We are stunned. We had thought we would not be able to see Benjamin for two more days. Here we are, just arrived at the hotel—just landed in the country—talking to someone we have never heard of who says she is about to bring us to our son. Jan calls back to say it will be thirty minutes instead of twenty, and we have just recovered enough to ask what we would be doing at the orphanage—visiting? No, *picking him up!* We could take him with us today, then go back for the adoption legalities on Monday.

Quick! We dig out gifts for the orphanage from among the mess of broken baby food jars. What should we bring for Benjamin? Where is the camera? We quickly change clothes, brush teeth, and change some American dollars into Vietnamese dong. We pause just enough to appreciate the irony of this frantic rushing after so many creeping months of waiting.

Then we are off for a wild, gloriously exciting ride, out from Ho Chi Minh City into the countryside province of Benjamin's orphanage. We resist the pull of the mesmerizing

panorama out the window and ask Ms. Jan for all she knows
about our boy. We also ask her some questions about her life
and work, finding her to be warm and engaging, thoughtful and quite proficient in English. After about an hour, our
driver pulls into the gated compound of the orphanage. Jan
leads us through a dusty courtyard to a staircase, around, up,
and to a room at the top. The first person we glimpse in that
room is a small boy standing alone, framed in the doorway.
We recognize him immediately. Our Benjamin. The time of
separation has just ended.

Our union with Benjamin is a jumble. In the periphery
of our minds, we note that there are several caretakers and
about fifteen children in the room, mostly babies and toddlers,
some lying awake in metal cribs. We want to focus completely
on Benjamin but are self-conscious. Everyone is watching us,
and we wonder what we are supposed to say and do. The caretakers are talking to Benjamin, telling him to go to us, we guess.
We have brought candy for the children, so Jan takes a Tootsie
Roll Pop, opens it and shows it to Benjamin, then hands it
to Phil, who picks up Benjamin and gives him the lollipop.
Benjamin looks a bit overwhelmed, but he does not cry, and a
few minutes later he indicates by arms and voice that he does
not want Phil to put him down. I wish I could take more
pictures of this most important moment, of the caretakers, of
this room my son has been living in, but I feel awkward, not
knowing what is expected of us, not wanting to make a fuss.

We play for a few minutes with the other children, try to
interact with their caretakers without a common language; we
distribute candy and bubbles. Then Jan leads us out and back
to the car. It feels ironic again—after months and months of
laborious paperwork, resubmission of paperwork that had ex-
pired during the wait, and walls of resistance in trying to get
this child, here we are just picking him up and walking away
with him without any formalities.

Once in the car, the awkwardness vanishes. It feels perfectly natural to have Benjamin on our laps. We give him toys to play with and are delighted to see how he interacts with something new, trying to figure out how it works. He remains stoic all the way through the departure from the orphanage and into the car (how few times he has probably been in a car), out of the car and up the stairs into the hotel. But trauma finally overtakes Benjamin when we enter the elevator. I have a new perspective on the fearsomeness of an elevator—a small room with a door that appears from the side, and mysteriously closes and traps you inside. I sympathize with Benjamin's howls.

Back in our room, in the midst of hastily thrown open suitcases, we watch our new son intently. He experiences his first disposable diapers, a bath, toys, new foods. We rejoice and marvel that he is with us. After months of waiting and now, all of a sudden, we are living with a boy named Benjamin.

That evening, still in a happy whirlwind, we use the hotel's computer to write to our daughters and family and friends, telling them about our surprising, wonderful day. I type quickly to help Phil—who would have thought that tonight he would be trying to keep his exploratory toddler from damaging the hotel's office equipment? I smile in happy wonder. My hastily written e-mail ends:

"He certainly is a boy! First smile came when banging two unlikely things together, first laugh from throwing rubber duckies. He thinks books are bats for hitting balls. He's had Cheerios, a bath, and his first power struggle with his parents (over electrical outlets). We are enraptured. Phil's proclaimed that he will be an engineer—he's into problem solving and exploring. As far as we can tell, he is robust and doing well in all ways. We are a bit stunned and thankful. No time for jet lag!"

ADOPTED

Journal Entry: Monday, November 8, 5:15 a.m.:

Benjamin cried about an hour ago. We went to the crib, where he was standing, and I picked him up. He settled right away and fell asleep lying on my chest. Later, when he was in the bed between us, he would reach out his hand, which I'd hold or put against my cheek, and he'd roll towards me. What special joy to be able to comfort him—something I've wanted to do for so long.

In a room of a hotel in swirling Ho Chi Minh City is a newly forming family. Like most new parents, we are enraptured with our child, eagerly sharing with each other the little discoveries we make about him. We have the camera out often and love to make him smile and laugh. We even think it's delightful when he drops the tennis ball into the toilet. We also enjoy interacting with the hotel staff, including its manager, an energetic British man experienced with newly adopted children. He motorbikes to the store to buy prunes, which he takes to the hotel's small kitchen to create a concoction sure to help traumatized toddlers' sluggish digestive tracts.

Two days after our right-off-the-plane union with Benjamin we return to the orphanage to complete his official adoption. We dress up nicely, as recommended, and pack gifts for the orphanage director and caretakers. We enjoy lively conversation in the car with the congenial Jan, listening to the stories of her family's experiences during and after the war. We are interested in her insight on the current state of men, women, and marriage in Vietnam.

At the orphanage we step out of the car into a flurry of greeting, not for us, we sense, but for Benjamin. Several women stand in the courtyard; one reaches for Benjamin and takes him from our arms, talking to him in happy chatter, and then whisks him off into the inner building.

Taken aback, I watch Benjamin going up the stairs to his old room, not knowing if I should follow. We notice a small building that opens into the courtyard. It is filled with a long table, set with tea and snacks; apparently they planned for us to all sit at the table and have refreshments together. But Benjamin, in the courtyard, is creating too much excitement. He is encircled by half a dozen women, who seem to be talking to and about him. We stand outside the circle, in the door of the tea room, watching. I feel like an intruder, a rich American with fancy clothes, coming to take Benjamin away from people who seem to have genuine affection for him.

The rest of the afternoon swirls with confused emotion and activity. We leave the orphanage once to go to the justice department, the orphanage director following on his motorbike; we return. We leave again to go to the immigration police; we return. Only dimly do we know what we are doing. At the justice department, it seems that we are signing multiple copies of the papers that make us legally Benjamin's parents—all I could read as the papers flew by was something about taking the rights and responsibilities of parents.

Before the signing, we wait outside on the long porch of the court building among petitioners who mill around waiting, and we wonder whether it is a culturally appropriate place to change Benjamin's diaper. During the signing we are preoccupied with how to keep Benjamin happy and quiet. Whenever we hand him a toy, he promptly drops it, sending it rolling under the desk and to the feet of the somber judge.

At the immigration department, a few low, gray buildings among disheveled grounds, we sign the papers to apply for

Benjamin's passport. Again, we are fully occupied trying to keep Benjamin quiet. A large Vietnamese flag hangs behind the officer's desk; in front of the flag is a bust of Ho Chi Minh, "Uncle Ho," bringer of communism to Vietnam and the national hero. Benjamin, alarmed by the statue, raises his arm towards it in apparent defiance. We gently pull his arm down, lest our boy's gesture offend the immigration police.

We walk out of the immigration office, damp with sweat, trying to keep our balance as we pick our way through broken cement rubble while hanging on to Benjamin, his stuffed diaper bag and our backpack full of money and paperwork. Several uniformed men scrutinize us as we walk by. It is hard to tell if they are on duty and guarding us or just milling around. We sit in the car, making small talk with the driver for a few long minutes while Jan tries to smooth out a problem. We still do not know what is happening but trust she does, as we have trusted all afternoon when she disappears and reappears, telling us where to go and what to do. She comes back. All our paperwork has been sent into the system. We hope it will emerge in several days with Benjamin's passport attached.

Now we are back at the orphanage for the third time today. Jan has fluttered off somewhere. We are again awkward and unsure. Earlier in the day we had gone up to Benjamin's old room. Caretakers watched us interact with the children, cautiously at first, then more freely. I popped up and down the sides of cribs, eliciting giggles by playing peek-a-boo. Phil played with two smiling girls, about seven years old, who seemed happy to dance with him. It felt like a privilege to spend time with these orphaned children. We stayed until Jan summoned us to sign papers.

This time, still not sure what to do with ourselves, we follow Benjamin (someone has taken him again) back to a long, outdoor table where some of the older children are eating. We watch an elderly caretaker dole out some sort of stew from a huge iron pot in the middle of the table. The children seem to have a range of physical and mental impairments. A boy with a stellar smile hops around on what is left of his amputated legs. Some of the children can only speak in grunts, but try to communicate with us. A girl with no obvious physical impairment sits in bed staring blankly out the window.

The caretaker serving the meal uses sign language to tell us when Benjamin takes his naps. She gives us some other tips that we can't understand about how to take care of him. We are touched by her desire to help us know Benjamin. As we slowly shed our awkwardness, I sit on the bench and pick up a spoon to help a teenage boy who is unable to feed himself. But then we are told that it is time to go.

The orphanage director is next to the car holding Benjamin, seemingly reluctant to have him leave. We give this dignified, kind-looking man a gift and ask Jan to translate as we thank him for his work and tell him that we are grateful for the care Benjamin has had at his first home. He says he knows that the second home will be better. We clasp hands.

I wonder what it is like to direct a Vietnamese orphanage, to care for children, advocate for their release, and then watch them go off with strangers. How can we communicate how momentous this day is to us by giving someone a pen set and stammering a few hastily translated words? Does this man, like us, want to cross cultures and language to communicate his heart? Or does he just smile and tolerate these foreigners as a necessary part of his job? I wish we knew him better. He invites us to come back to visit while we are waiting for clearance to leave the country. It is an appealing invitation. We would like to spend more time with the children. But we know that we do not belong here. Today we have felt like intrusive Americans. And we think it would be best to stay away in order to spare Benjamin the stress of going in and out of this place.

For our dear little boy is falling apart. As we step into the car, the director hands us a crying Benjamin. Today this boy has gone to and from the orphanage so many times and been held by so many different people that now he is in confused turmoil; we also are feeling it. We have prayed earnestly these last two years that God would provide people to genuinely care for Benjamin. Today we have seen answers to those prayers. It seems that Benjamin is well liked at the orphanage; today he was positively doted on. We know this is not always the case at orphanages, and we are humbly touched to see God's faithfulness to Benjamin. But the attachments mean tears now, and a difficult parting. As we pull away from the orphanage our hearts are filled with the distress of our son, the sadness of those watching him leave, and the plight of the many other children who will not be leaving. Tears in our eyes, we are both thinking of the promise of Jesus to come back and redeem his creation. We long for it to be soon.

In the middle of this tumultuous day, the law confirmed what God had started. We have adopted Benjamin. He is our son.

GRAFTING

It is our fifth day with Benjamin. We marvel at his presence and rejoice that this enormous change in his life has begun. Yet this shift from orphanage to family brings with it some sorrow, and waves of sadness come over me.

I am sad that Benjamin is often so somber and fearful, especially when we are out. He is not carefree as a toddler boy should be. He clings to us, his face often clouded with a furrowed brow. He rarely smiles outside the hotel room. One day, at the urging of our hotel's enthusiastic doorman, we venture into a taxi to visit a large park on the outskirts of the city. As we stroll through sights that would delight most toddlers—fountains, statues, sparrows—Benjamin often grunts and raises his arm as if to defend himself. He has been confined within the walls of one room in an orphanage for so long, and now that he is out he does not know that he is safe and can freely enjoy these colors and shapes and sounds.

I am sad that he does not respond to his new name or things we say because he does not understand our words. Before this week, he had probably not heard the name of Jesus, and he is not familiar with the dozens of songs and games that our daughters knew by this age from the simple immersion of life together. At nearly two years old he has never had anyone to call Papa and Mama, and he doesn't seem to expect meaningful interaction with us. We communicate some with sign language and tone of voice. But it's odd to say: "Benjamin, look!" or "Benjamin, where is your Papa?" when he doesn't even look up from what he is doing. I can usually interact with children this age, even when they are not my own, and enjoy more mutual understanding. Our communication with Benjamin feels so limited in comparison.

I am sad to not know what is underneath Benjamin's behavior. Why did he cling to his bowl of oatmeal last night, carrying it everywhere, putting it down for a bit, then picking it up, looking at it, mixing it, tasting? Was it fascination with a new food? Or that he never had the freedom of holding his own food at the orphanage? Was it a sense of security and control in being able to grasp something in a time of upheaval? Or did they wander around with food at the orphanage and not have set times and places for eating? Maybe he has he been hungry and thus clings to and hoards food when he has opportunity (as we have read sometimes happens with orphans after being transferred to families). Why does he raise his arm when he is afraid? Has he been physically abused? Has he needed to defend himself? I have dozens of questions that I cannot answer.

Parents can often interpret their child's behavior because they have been together so much. We do not have a shared language or history with Benjamin to help us understand him. We are groping and guessing on both sides. It is obviously best for children to be born into a stable family and grow up in it, so they grow easily and naturally into so many things. I have thought in terms of trying to make up for lost time; now I feel more acutely that there really has been precious time lost, time that can not be recovered.

Benjamin, too, has to go through this pain of being grafted into a family. We do trust the results will be worth it, but there is pain now, pain for him to be torn away from what he knows and start over, suddenly living with people whose language he has never heard, at an age at which no one can explain it to him. He cannot express the trouble in his soul with words, but we see a bit of it in other ways— in his raised arm and the moans in his crib.

I am saddened to tears now because Benjamin is moaning in his sleep as I watch over his nap. I seek comfort from God's word:

Arise, Lord! Lift up your hand, O God. Do not forget the helpless. Why does the wicked man revile God? Why does he say to himself 'He won't call me to account?' But you, O God, do see trouble and grief, you consider it to take it in hand. The victim commits himself to you; you are the helper of the fatherless. You hear, O Lord, the desire of the afflicted; you encourage them, and you listen to their cry, defending the fatherless and the oppressed, in order that man, who is of the earth, may terrify no more.

—Psalm 10:12-14,17–18

This passage lifts a burden from me as I sit on the bed reading while Benjamin moans in his sleep. I can cry out to the Lord with the words of those who have gone before me. I can appeal to God to arise, to show his mercy to the weak and needy. I can ask the God who has revealed himself as a father to the fatherless to lift up his hand on Benjamin's behalf, to hear his moans, to protect and defend him. I can cry out to him with passion on Benjamin's behalf, and on behalf of the other orphans I saw in the orphanage, and all the orphans around the world. I can appeal to God's character as he has revealed it in the Bible.

I have been feeling inadequate to the looming work of helping Benjamin integrate into the family. It is an enormous job, and I fear not being able to do it well. But what I most want to do—protect, defend, and uplift this boy—is ultimately God's work. I am invited to participate, but I do not bear ultimate responsibility. God says that he himself will listen to, encourage and lift up the fatherless and oppressed.

And not only does God say he is the defender of the afflicted and defenseless; he says he reserves special honor for them. Jesus said that those who mourn are blessed because they will be comforted. Isaiah prophesied that the Messiah would "comfort all who mourn, and provide for those who grieve in Zion—to bestow on them a crown of beauty instead of ashes, the oil of gladness instead of mourning, and a garment of praise instead of a spirit of despair. They will be called oaks of righteousness, a planting of the LORD for the display of his splendor" (Is 61:1—3).

Our Lord loves to transform mourning into joy and brokenness into beauty. A mother from thousands of years ago, Hannah, saw it: "He raises the poor from the dust and lifts the needy from the ash heap; he seats them with princes and has them inherit a throne of honor." (1 Sm 2:8). Now we see his fulfillment of these promises only dimly; in eternity we will see how, around the world and throughout history, God has brought special honor and blessing and beauty to those who were vulnerable and poor and suffering. And we will glorify him for it.

I need to believe that the first twenty months of Benjamin's life were not all loss, that prayers have been and will be answered that God has used this time to create something beautiful. I need to believe that even this pain of being grafted into a new family can be redeemed, clothed with glorious garments of praise. I draw hope from the Lord who takes what is broken and makes it beautiful. It may take a long time. Oak trees grow slowly. But perhaps it is from the scars of Benjamin's broken places that a sapling is starting to grow, an oak of righteousness to display God's splendor.

BRINGING IN THE SHEAF

It is November 19, over two weeks since we left home. Yesterday, late in the afternoon, we landed in Los Angeles, bleary from hours upon hours of traveling with a toddler but basking still in the special moments of this journey. The immigration officer, after processing Benjamin's visa, welcomed him, calling him a new Yankee. We took him to McDonalds for his first U.S. meal, where he happily discovered french fries. We are cherishing every detail of this trip, but also longing to be home, to be united with our daughters and friends and start our life as a family of five.

Today Benjamin will fly home with us. Our bodies hum with excitement and jet lag; we are awake for hours before the early morning departure from our hotel to the airport. What praise and joy could be too high for this day of homecoming we have so longed for and were so helplessly unable to bring about? There will doubtless be more tears later, more trials around the bend of which we are now unaware. There will be times again that our song extolling the Lord is purely of faith, not sight. But not today. Today it is the sight that glorifies the Lord—the real body of a small boy, brought by God's hand into the love of a family and community.

I look through my Bible for something appropriate to mark the day. I find it—Benjamin's homecoming psalm.

When the Lord brought back the captives to Zion,
we were like men who dreamed.
Our mouths were filled with laughter,
our tongues with songs of joy.

Then it was said among the nations,
"The Lord has done great things for them."
The Lord has done great things for us,
and we are filled with joy.
Restore our fortunes, O Lord
like streams in the Negev.
Those who sow in tears will reap with songs of joy.
He who goes out weeping, carrying seed to sow,
will return with songs of joy, carrying sheaves
with him.

—Psalm 126

The person who wrote this psalm had once experienced a joyful deliverance which he calls to mind to help him persevere in his current trial. He asserts with faith that tearful sowing will someday lead to joyful harvest. Today we reap. We have sown prayer and labor for Benjamin in tears. Now we return with songs of joy, carrying our sheaf of a toddler boy with us.

The rest of the day is glorious. I exalt in flying across the country, moving closer and closer to reunion with my dearly missed girls while Benjamin sleeps on my lap. As we descend into Detroit through storm clouds we hear a crashing boom and feel a jolt as the plane is hit by lightning. The crew looks grave. It is the punctuating drama of a spectacular few weeks.

We touch down in Detroit, so far now from Vietnam. We are at the very back of a huge planeload of people. Seconds drag, and the people in front of us seem like they will not move; never have I so wanted to disembark a plane. Finally released, we race down the ramp into the arms of our daughters, parents, and friends. Benjamin, reluctant to be wakened, comes out of his shock by batting at the balloons brought in his honor. He shyly warms up to his sisters as they offer him lollipops, an echo of his first meeting with us a few days earlier. We make our way in a happy daze to retrieve our luggage, swept along in the care of others.

We have warned the girls that the enormous and abrupt changes in Benjamin's life will likely make him afraid or distant from them at first. They are eager to dote on him after months of pent-up sisterly affection, and we do not want them to be disappointed. Our concerns seem to be realized on the ride home; Benjamin is restrained in a car seat for the first time in his life and wails in fearful protest.

But to our utter joy, as soon as we reach our festively decorated home, Benjamin seems perfectly at ease. He races around in circles with his new sisters, laughing with them as he holds his balloons. The serious countenance of all of his orphanage photos turns into a boyish smile. The clouded scowl he wore during much of our time together in Vietnam changes into the radiance of someone happy to be loved and to be home. Our months of frustration, insecurity, worry, and waiting melt away.

"He knows he's home," says Phil, as we watch Benjamin chasing his sisters. I stare at my son, wonder filling my heart.

The Lord has done great things for us, and we are filled with joy. We have returned with songs of joy, carrying our precious sheaf with us.

GLORIA

It is advent, one month after Benjamin's homecoming. Our family of five lingers around the candle-lit dinner table after eating, and we spontaneously sing. The ascending and descending rolls of "Gloria in Excelsis Deo" in "Angels We Have Heard on High" are favorites of the girls (and their mother), and we sing it boisterously. Wide-eyed Benjamin watches with wonder, apparently taken aback by the outburst. He stares intently, candlelight reflecting off his face.

The look on that face tugs my memory back to Ho Chi Minh City. We had spent several hours one day with a guide from Vietnam Travel. Mr. Phong deftly moved us through the teeming city. He explained the relics at a historical museum, walked us along a bustling downtown street, and escorted us to a lacquerware factory to look over the shoulders of artisans. We tried to converse with our guide while managing the needs of an active, nervous toddler who was adjusting to his new parents and new life.

After lunch we drove through masses of motorbikes to Ho Chi Minh City's Chinatown, where Mr. Phong wanted to show us a Buddhist temple. We left the blaze of afternoon sun and entered the shadowed building, walking back through a series of dark rooms. Through air thick with incense we saw glints of dimly gleaming gold statues. Mr. Phong explained the system—you can purchase a coil of incense to be burned in the temple to secure protection or good fortune. The gods will grant favor as long as the coil burns. The ceiling was full of these slowly burning coils, each one representing a person trying to secure divine favor. Mr. Phong went to buy himself a coil while we tried to stand inconspicuously among men and women who shuffled around the dark room or bowed towards the statues, carrying out their transactions with blank faces. I wondered if there was any joy for them in this worship, wondered what kind of relationship they were seeking with their gods.

The Vietnamese culture has assimilated bits and pieces from Buddhism, Hinduism, Confucianism, Taoism, ancestor worship, and animism. This gives people a full spectrum of gods and spirits to placate. There is fear of ghosts and fear of being harmed by malignant spells. There are lucky and unlucky days, numbers, and gifts. Ancestors must be honored on certain days. Spirits abide everywhere and need to be kept happy.

At the temple, Benjamin was wide-eyed and serious, as he would be a month later at our dining room table. Everything outside his room at the orphanage was new to him, and he was trying to understand this larger world. We did not yet have a language in common, but he pointed toward everything as if wanting us to explain. We took a photo of him pointing up towards the rows of smoldering incense coils. It froze the moment in time. My thoughts from that moment are also preserved. I felt heavy to see these people trying to buy temporary favor from gods while so thankful that Benjamin would have the opportunity to come to know the God of love and forgiveness, life and joy.

How grateful I am that my relationship with God comes through Christ's work and not my diligence in religious activity. How grateful I am that, once given, God's forgiveness does not need to be purchased again, that it will not lapse when the incense coil burns out. His love, once set on us, can never be removed. "Day after day every priest stands and performs his religious duties; again and again he offers the same sacrifices, which can never take away sins. But when this priest had offered for all time one sacrifice for sins, he sat down at the right hand of God" (Heb 10:11–12). Jesus said that it was finished as he died on the cross, and it is still finished thousands of years later.

I am set in the light of God's favor, not by completing religious ceremonies, but by the sacrificial life and death of Jesus on my behalf. This work is complete and eternal. Because of this I am set free to adore and praise God, to enjoy him and sing heartily.

Now Benjamin has joined us around the table, again with eyes wide open, again trying to absorb the new things in his world. Just a few weeks after standing awkwardly in a Buddhist temple, I sit on the other side of the world, singing to the Lord with my husband and children. I rejoice at the glory of Jesus with the angels. And I rejoice at the beginning transformation that I see. Benjamin is in a different place, meeting a different God. He is soaking up what surrounds him with all his senses. I am deeply thankful that, at this moment, it is candlelight and carols.

Gloria in Excelsis Deo.

INTERLUDE

After Benjamin is safely home, we have a little time to breathe, to reflect on all that happened during the emotional tumult of the last two years. We have learned that this journey of adoption is not just a way to add children to our family, but also offers rich opportunity for us to know and embrace the Lord in fresh ways. In this short season of reflection, we try to absorb what has passed. We are also being prepared, though we do not yet know it, to bring another son home.

GREAT IS THY FAITHFULNESS

It was Thanksgiving Sunday when we first took Benjamin to church. The songs that morning were about God's faithfulness to all generations. I had sung these songs by faith for two years, desperately praying and hoping that God was going to show his great goodness to Benjamin. Finally, this tangible evidence of God's faithfulness gazed around the church from my arms. I declared "Great is Thy Faithfulness" with full voice, exalting in this triumphant finale to Benjamin's homecoming.

It was a glorious, victorious morning—for me. But standing right next to me, Phil found he could not sing these songs about God's faithfulness. He was deeply shaken by his visit to Vietnam, still feeling the weight of poverty and spiritual darkness he witnessed there. While standing, surrounded by music, in Thanksgiving worship, he was thinking of the children we had to leave behind at the orphanage. He thought of the row of metal cribs lining a stark room, and of the girl who stared blankly out a window. He remembered ragged men sleeping on the streets, children begging, burdened-looking people slowly pedaling bicycles through the city, and small shrines to buddhas set up in restaurants and hotel lobbies. Though he was as thankful as I to have Benjamin home, he grieved for the many others. Being in a congregation full of secure, happy people intensified rather than alleviated his distress. Phil and I had gone through this journey together, but now we perceived the same events differently: I saw God's victory in bringing Benjamin home; he saw the hopelessness of a broken world.

In the happy-ending weeks after Benjamin's homecoming, we often marveled at how well he was adjusting, at the radiance of his expression compared to the photos from his orphanage days, and at the delight he and his sisters gave each other. We, together with our friends, celebrated all that God had done to bring Benjamin into our family. But through this happy time, Phil also struggled. His time in Vietnam had disturbed him deeply.

Vietnam is one of the poorest countries in the world. Its people have been wounded by colonialism, war, communism, natural disasters, and poverty, and weakened by international isolation. Military and government leaders abuse their power and brutally repress minorities and others. The Vietnamese people, many struggling to survive, have very little access to the Christian message that could give them hope, and as with other communist nations, Christians are sometimes bullied, imprisoned, and tortured for their faith. Missionary work is officially prohibited.

How staggering to think of those few suffering individuals that we saw, multiplied throughout a country, and throughout the world—for Vietnam is not alone in its devastating problems, including its repression of Christianity. Many other countries know similar anguish.

A glimpse of this suffering shook the foundation of Phil's faith and made him question God, who seemed to have abandoned the Vietnamese. How could God make parents choose between putting their children in an orphanage or letting them starve? How could he allow those children to grow up without families and then be sent out to live on the streets, with no one to give them hope?

Phil told some respected friends of his crisis of faith and asked for their thoughts about how God can tolerate this kind of brokenness throughout a country. These brothers listened carefully and compassionately to his struggle. One friend responded that perhaps God was letting Phil into his confidence in a new way, intentionally opening his eyes to more of the world's pain. It is a privilege to break out of our small, sheltered world. It is a privilege to be touched, and not hardened, by seeing things in the world a little bit more as God sees them. Perhaps Phil's pain was molding him to be more like Jesus, who has experienced all of our suffering, and preparing him for some future work.

During a long evening's conversation with other friends, we thought about the origin of evil that led to this massive devastation. God could have prevented anything bad from ever entering his creation, but he didn't. He let it in. We concluded, with incomplete understanding, that it must be better this way. Maybe God is more glorified by redeeming brokenness than by creating unmarred perfection. Part of the glory of Jesus is that he was slain and resurrected to redeem us, a redemption that would not have been necessary had there been no sin and no suffering.

Over several months of these conversations and others, Phil slowly came back to full confidence in the Lord. The incomplete answers that encouraged him may not be the same explanations that help someone else, but they are significant to us because they brought him back to faith in God. Phil worked through his crisis of faith alongside others. I tried to support him in his turmoil but was limited in my ability to help; I am thankful that he could turn to others and that through them his trust in God was renewed.

God turned the trials of this adoption into special opportunities for us to work through our beliefs. While waiting for Benjamin, I had struggled in confidence about prayer, a struggle Phil did not share. On our trip to Vietnam, I had seen the same things as Phil but had not been so distressed in my faith; nor had Phil been so disturbed by his past exposures to poverty and spiritual darkness. For his own reasons, God allowed Phil to feel the pain of the lost world this time and to grapple with its implications. Over time, Phil's crisis enriched him. It triggered other memories and emotions and led to healing, understanding, and more freedom in his walk with the Lord. This struggle was a precious part of God's faithfulness to him.

I struggled to understand prayer; Phil struggled to trust God in spite of the poverty in Vietnam. Through this adoption journey, God was leading us each through a personal valley. These valleys were essential on our pilgrimage paths that led us closer to God. I cherish them now as part of the enduring, unexpected legacy of our adoption of children.

All who choose to enter an adoption choose to open themselves to pain. We can choose to embrace the grief inherent in the journey, letting it mold us to be more like Jesus. We need not deny pain. We need not oversimplify complex questions. We need not fear when something in God's word or world is difficult to understand or embrace. These heart-struggles can push us to new ground in our relationship with God. May we be given grace to accept such struggles when they come, and not shrink back from where the Lord wants to bring us. In both joy and grief, may we recognize the gifts he offers us. Though it may be hard to sing in the thick of distress, at the end we will certainly look back and declare "Great Is Thy Faithfulness."

FACETS OF PRAYER

Several weeks after our return home with Benjamin, I had lunch with Diane, the teacher of our weekly fellowship for mothers. She asked me how I had resolved my confusion about prayer, triggering my realization that I had not come to a satisfying answer to those questions of half a year earlier. So I asked Diane, again, to talk about the prayer promises with our mothers' group.

Later, Diane called me to ask if *I* would speak to the ladies about the prayer promises at next week's meeting. I was baffled by her request. I thought she must have misunderstood me, thinking that I knew more than I really did. I insisted to her that I was really confused about this topic and could only offer questions. She convinced me to at least pray and consider her suggestion, but I hung up befuddled. How could I speak to others about prayer when I so very much wanted someone to teach me? Why did Diane seem so confident that I had something helpful to share?

As I lay awake in bed, I had an idea—and another, and another. During the next days threads of understanding about our years of praying for Benjamin knit themselves together in my mind. I hurried to write down the new thoughts; to my amazement I did indeed talk about prayer at the meeting the next week.

The picture that has helped me since that wakeful night is one of facets. "When the light of gospel passes through the prism of biblical language we find that it is broken up into many constituent parts, each with its own beauty and glory."[12] This idea, applied to prayer, helped me through my confusion. Different passages in the Bible look at the diamond of prayer from different sides, breaking the whole into its constituent parts. I was frustrated when I tried to fit all the teaching on prayer into one mold, as if trying to push all facets of a diamond onto one surface. We cannot comprehend all the aspects of prayer if we try to see them together, but we can appreciate the beauty of each when we consider it separately.

Three facets of prayer stood out to me. The first is father-child prayer. Some passages about prayer focus on us coming to God as our Father. The Sermon on the Mount is rich with these pictures of prayer; Jesus says that prayer should be like going into a private room to talk to our Father (Mt 6:6), and that we should even address our prayers to "Our Father." He reminds us what it is like to care for our children: "Which of you, if his son asks for bread, will give him a stone? Or if he asks for a fish, will give him a snake? If you, then, though you are evil, know how to give good gifts to your children, how much more will your Father in heaven give good gifts to those who ask him!" (Mt 7:9–11)

When we consider this side of prayer, we see that God will provide for us because he is our loving and wise Father. Prayer is trusting conversation with a Father who delights in giving good gifts to his children. He promises to bring what is best for us even when we cannot discern what that is.

I reflected on our wait for Benjamin. All the prayers we made for him had their source in one root desire: that God would love Benjamin and care for him. Our cries for God to send Benjamin to us were really cries for God to take care of him, to be a good Father to him. We thought the best way for God to love him was to bring him to his waiting family.

We can see now that God has answered these prayers, and even in part by not sending him home right away. Because Benjamin was in an orphanage in Vietnam for so long, and because we had no way to bring him home, we kept praying intensely for him. Others were also drawn to this little boy and prayed for his body and soul. I do not remember praying so fervently for my girls when they were that age; they were with us, and we felt more secure about their health and safety. Our desperation for Benjamin drew out many prayers that will bear fruit throughout his life. God was setting his Fatherly love on Benjamin that whole time by calling people to pray for him. A second facet is prayer that aligns us with God's will. In the garden of Gesthemane, Jesus prayed, "My Father, if it is possible, may this cup be taken from me." He kept praying this, sweating blood with the struggle of it, until he was able to say "yet not my will but yours be done." There are other prayers of this kind recorded in the Scriptures. Paul the apostle had a "thorn in the flesh" that he asked three times for God to remove. God did not remove it, and finally Paul said he could delight in and boast about his weaknesses and hardships, because they resulted in God being glorified (2 Cor 12:4–8). King David and other authors of the psalms struggled similarly in prayer, moving from agitation to peace, from crying out for God to remove affliction to trusting God in the midst of the affliction.

This kind of prayer involves honest wrestling with God that ends in the petitioner being able to sincerely say, "Thy will be done." It does not only happen over dramatic, life-uprooting issues; it can just as easily apply in mundane, day-to-day frustrations. If I am feeling restless, discontent, or irritable, my questions to God (spoken or unspoken) are the same: "Why are you letting this happen? Why are my children this way? Please change my situation, remove this trial." These can be opportunities for me to keep coming back to God until I reach a place of wholeheartedly embracing his will.

We knew that our wait for Benjamin was as much about our growth in faith as it was about getting our son home. The pain of it not going as we wanted flushed issues out of my heart that wouldn't have been exposed otherwise: Do I really trust God? Will I trust his love no matter what happens? I engaged in several rounds of this wrestling, and, though it was painful, I was thankful for how the questions exposed my weak faith and allowed me to join with others—from throughout history—in praying that God's will would be mine.

A third facet of prayer is that of master and servants. This is the kind of prayer that confused me during the long wait for Benjamin, the type that has at least one expansive promise in each of the gospels, such as in Matthew 17:20: "I tell you the truth, if you have faith as small as a mustard seed, you can say to this mountain, 'Move from here to there' and it will move. Nothing will be impossible for you." (*see also* Mk 11:23–24, Lk 17:6, Jn 15:7)

Bearing fruit that glorifies God is at the heart of this type of prayer. There is a partnership between God, the Master and we the servants, as he weaves our prayers in with his kingdom work. The focus is not on our needs but on God's work in the world. There are conditions in these promises: We need to pray while abiding in the Lord, with faith, in his name, and with right motive. When the conditions are met, he will fulfill his promises to answer those prayers. As we spend time with him we will be able to discern how to pray.

Did we meet the conditions of this kind of prayer as we prayed for Benjamin? I hope that the answer was yes, that our prayers for Benjamin were made while abiding in the Lord, as partners with him on Benjamin's behalf. I think this explains why we couldn't let go of Benjamin when it seemed more reasonable to try to adopt another child.

One of the conditions for master-servant prayer is that the prayers be made with faith. Faith is being sure of what we hope for and certain of what we do not see (Heb 11:1). To pray with faith must then mean that we sometimes will not see the answer, at least not immediately. We did not see the result of our prayer for Benjamin for many months; then the veil was lifted and we glimpsed how God had been fulfilling those prayers for Benjamin's protection all along. Sometimes the time of not seeing lasts much longer, but mysteriously, invisibly, the Lord is fulfilling the prayers that we offer in his name.

We can also be assured that Jesus himself prays for us. While we falter and stumble in our prayers, he is always alive to act as our great high priest. He intercedes for us with perfect constancy, love, and wisdom (Heb 7:25). How that can inspire us to pray with perseverance and hope!

God uses our prayer to care for his children, to work his will into our hearts, and to do his work in the world; he fuses these facets together to create a sparkling diamond of prayer.

ORPHANS AND WIDOWS

Religion that God our Father accepts
as pure and faultless is this:
to look after orphans and widows in their distress
and to keep oneself from being polluted by the world.

James 1:27

Our Bible study group decided to study adoption, and we started with a survey of what the Bible says about orphans. Time after time, Old Testament prophets pleaded with the Israelites to care for the oppressed—specifically for the orphans, widows, and foreigners in their midst. They warned the people that their relationship with God and protection from him was at risk, in part because they disregarded the poor: "Stop bringing meaningless offerings! Your incense is detestable to me ... When you spread out your hands in prayer, I will hide my eyes from you; even if you offer many prayers, I will not listen ... Seek justice, encourage the oppressed. Defend the cause of the fatherless, plead the case of the widow." (Is 1:13, 15, 17)

Through many similar passages, we see that the vitality of our relationship with God is connected to our advocacy for the destitute. But God leaves undefined the specifics of how to care for orphans. As our small group studied this topic we noted the small number of non-blood-relative adoptions in the Old Testament. Extended families generally took care of their widows and orphans. A widowed woman without children was supposed to be married to her husband's brother or other kinsman so that she would be provided for and the family line would be preserved. If there was no extended family then the whole community was responsible—God told the

Israelites to leave food in the fields for orphans and other poor and to include them in holiday celebrations.

In the ancient world, a childless couple sometimes had the husband conceive a child with his wife's servant. The baby would then be "adopted" by husband and wife, while the birth mother apparently lived alongside. The story of Jacob, Rachel, and Leah and their servants in Genesis 30 is an emotion-packed example of this method of building a family. This kind of adoption seems strange to us. But the people of ancient Israel would find equally bizarre our tradition of choosing a stranger from across the country or the world, completely unrelated by blood, and adopting him or her into our family.

With the New Testament, we have another incentive to care for orphans: We want to be like Jesus. He identified with the poor and outcast. He also received and blessed children in a way that was radical in his time. Orphans are children—and they are usually poor—so we can follow Jesus by loving them. Soon after Jesus walked on earth, his disciples started imitating their teacher by defending their culture's weakest members.

The early church was born into the Roman Empire. Roman fathers of that time had authority to decide if their newborn infants would live; babies that the fathers did not want were left at designated places outside the city walls to die of exposure or be eaten by wild animals. Greek and Roman thinkers of that time did not consider it wrong to kill children, but early in the life of the church, Christians spoke out against infanticide and started taking in abandoned babies. They influenced the empire.

In the 6th century, Emperor Justinian wrote that those who abandon their children should be prosecuted by law, and that "should exposure occur, the finder of the child is to see that he is baptized and that he is treated with Christian care and compassion. They may be adopted as *ad scriptitiorumae* even as we ourselves have been adopted into the kingdom of grace."[13]

God's people have continued to seek justice for children in ways fitting to their time and place in history. William Carey, missionary in India in the 18th century, labored to keep babies from being thrown into the Ganges River as sacrifices. Amy Carmichael, living in India a century later, adopted the girls who ran away from forced prostitution in Hindu temples.[14] Jesus told his disciples that they would always have the poor with them. The need has always been there, but our ways of meeting it change with time and culture, and with the creativity and resources God has given us. Each generation has unique opportunities that shape its response to God's mandate to care for orphans.

Our family's response has been to adopt children. In this season of our lives, we have chosen to pour much of ourselves into a very limited number of (former!) orphans.

But there are so many other creative ways to follow these broad mandates, ways open to us by the context of the time and place we live. We have a diverse, vibrant array of opportunities to serve the weak. Some can pray consistently for one child and some can engage in transforming the structural evils that perpetrate injustice. Some will bring foster children into their homes and some will bring their children to visit an elderly, lonely widow.

There are destitute and lonely people in orphanages across the world and also in our neighborhoods. There are single mothers in need of encouragement and help, children struggling to survive in the inner city, men and women languishing in nursing homes. Even in my limited sphere I see multiple, diverse ways to serve orphans, even apart from those who have come our way through the adoptions: through international child sponsorship programs, relationships in the inner-city, our church's missionaries. There are many places where we can share our resources in money, time, and prayer, participating with God in bringing justice to the oppressed.

With our adoptions, obedience to God's commands to care for orphans included trial and sacrifice. It cost a lot in money and time and emotional stress. But the difficulties have been far outweighed by the immeasurable blessing of having these precious boys in our family, and outweighed as well by the gifts that came in the process of adopting them, lessons that were sometimes painful but also priceless in leading us to deeper trust in the Lord. God's commands are both for his glory and for our good. When Moses prepared the nation to enter the promised land, he often prophetically cried out with God's desire that the people would obey the law for their own blessing: "Oh, that their hearts would be inclined to fear me and keep all my commands always, so that it might go well with them and their children forever!" (Dt 5:29). God asks us to help the helpless, not only for their sake, but also for ours.

"Is not this the kind of fasting I have chosen: to loose the chains of injustice and untie the cords of the yoke, to set the oppressed free and break every yoke? Is it not to share your food with the hungry and to provide the poor wanderer with shelter – when you see the naked, to clothe him, and not to turn away from your own flesh and blood? Then your light will break forth like the dawn, and your healing will quickly appear; then your righteousness will go before you, and the glory of the Lord will be your rear guard. Then you will call, and the Lord will answer; you will cry for help, and he will say: Here am I.

"If you do away with the yoke of oppressed, with the pointing finger and malicious talk, and if you spend your-selves in behalf of the hungry and satisfy the needs of the oppressed, then your light will rise in the darkness, and your night will become like the noonday. The Lord will guide you always; he will satisfy your needs in a sun-scorched land and will strengthen your frame. You will be like a well-watered garden, like a spring whose waters never fail." (Is 58:6–11)

Our God gives generously to us while we feebly try to give to him, and lets us find our life when we seem to be losing it. The Lord may ask me to give more sacrificially to orphans and widows and those in distress. If I do, I believe I will be drawn nearer to God and discover my worship enlivened and my life more full.

SAFELY HOME

Can a mother forget the baby at her breast
and have no compassions on the child she has borne?
Though she may forget, I will not forget you!
See, I have engraved you on the palms of my hands,
your walls are ever before me.

Isaiah 49:15–16

There are a few last, lingering remnants of paperwork: We put an ad in the local newspaper declaring our intention to officially change Benjamin's name. We apply for his social security card. Then, legally, our adoption is finished. And our life with Benjamin has just begun. We settle in for the long haul of parenting.

Benjamin seems to be doing well, but we are beginning to taste uncertainty. When he breaks out into distressed, difficult behavior (as all children sometimes do), we discover that we do not always know how to interpret it. Is it adoption-related? Is it the fallout of physical and emotional deprivation from years in an orphanage? It could be a genetic trait from his birth parents. Or it could be just because he is a boy (and I am only acquainted with girls), or because he did not sleep enough, or maybe he ate something that is upsetting his stomach. It is hard to know how to diagnose the ups and downs of his behavior.

We are learning how to be father and mother. Every time you become parent to another child, you have to learn again, because each child is different. This child's differences include elements new to us. The growth of adoption has prompted more medical and social professionals to help us understand those children and parent them well. These are valuable resources for adoptive families. But, there is no formula that fits all children (adopted or not) and gives us simple steps to curing all their problems. We feel more insecure when we want to be good parents but do not know how.

What does an ideal parent look like? Here is one description of a perfect father: "Faithful in love and care, generous and thoughtful, interested in all we do, respecting our individuality, skillful in training us, wise in guidance, always available, helping us to find ourselves in maturity, integrity, and uprightness."[15] This is how J.I. Packer described God. Our heavenly Father is the only perfect father. He is also an adoptive Father, and can be our inspiration and model as we parent our children. God's adoption of us can fuel us with great hope, and as we look to him we find wisdom to help us parent our children.

What does it mean to have God as our Father? First, our Father initiates our adoption. "In love he predestined us to be adopted as his sons through Jesus Christ, in accordance with his pleasure and will—to the praise of his glorious grace, which he has freely given us in the one he loves" (Eph 1:5–6). Before the world was even created God planned to adopt me. Just as we set our love on Benjamin before he was aware of it, so God set his love on us, not only before we were aware of it but before we were even born.

Orphaned children, weak and defenseless, cannot earn their way into a family. They cannot represent themselves as worthy of being adopted. The parents must take the initiative. God chose to adopt us. We are recipients of his initiating love, love that has come and sought us. We were unattractive and worse when he redeemed us from slavery and brought us into his home, and yet he drew near to us. We continue to be unattractive, and sometimes rebellious, and he still loves us.

Orphans first brought into a home, particularly if they are older, sometimes need to be consistently loved for a period of time before feeling secure. They may push against the people who love them, testing to see if the love will remain when met with bad behavior. Wise parents will steadfastly love their children despite this security-seeking resistance. They will use different means to bring assurance of their love: gentle touch, affirming words, gifts, consistency, and structure. They gradually teach children who have been orphaned how to live in a family.

So our God gives us his word and the Spirit of sonship to assure us that we are his children, that he loves us dearly and intends for us to be in his family. In Packer's words, "God will go out of His way to make His children feel His love for them, and know their privilege and security as members of His family. Adopted children need assurance that they belong, and a perfect parent will not withhold it."[16] How humbling it is that the Maker of the Universe would stoop to lavish love on me in a multitude of ways so that I will believe that he loves me, and learn how to be part of his family.

Our Father is wise and strong. His unlimited resources are combined with unerring wisdom and unshakeable love. He has the wisdom and riches to give us, always and exactly, what is for our best.

> Which of you, if his son asks for bread, will give him a stone? Or if he asks for a fish, will give him a snake? If you, then, though you are evil, know how to give good gifts to your children, how much more will your Father in heaven give good gifts to those who ask him! ... So do not worry, saying, 'What shall we eat?' or 'What shall we drink?' or 'What shall we wear?' For the pagans run after all these things, and your heavenly Father knows that you need them." (Mt 7:9–11, 6:31–32).

If food has been scarce over a period of time, it is natural to worry about it. Children who have been institutionalized may demonstrate this; even after being taken to a home where food is plentiful, they sometimes hoard and hide caches of it—probably as insurance, in case food is later taken away from them. How many ways do we do this as God's children? We grasp and horde, worry and fret. Our actions sometimes reveal that we do not entirely trust the care of our Father. As adoptive parents, we hope and pray that after years of faithful provision our children will not feel the need to hoard food or act in other fretful ways. Children of a good, rich father need not be anxious. They know that they are well cared for and are free to enjoy the life that he spreads out before them.

When we first had Benjamin with us, he had just been torn from all relationships he had known. For several weeks, his surroundings spun around him, from hotel to taxis, restaurants, offices, planes, and then a completely new continent. What he most needed to know was that we would always be with him, that though everything else changed, we would remain constant. We all have a built-in longing to not be deserted. My children will cling to me in the midst of their temper tantrums, desperately not wanting me to leave them alone. When Benjamin is older, he will sometimes say: "You don't love me when I'm bad," as if to receive the assurance, over and over, that I do.

The children's book *The Runaway Bunny* reveals our deep desire to not be abandoned. A baby rabbit talks about running away from his mother, and his mother always counters by telling him that she will follow him and win him back, until he finally concedes her permanent love and decides to just stay at home after all. The mother rabbit shows us a bit of God's pursuing love, we are all like the baby bunny who hides while secretly hoping to be found.

One of the last promises of Jesus to his disciples was "Surely I am with you always, to the very end of the age" (Mt 28:20). He will never abandon us. Our testimony is that, "neither death nor life, neither angels nor demons, neither the present nor the future, nor any powers, neither height nor depth, nor anything else in all creation, will be able to separate us from the love of God that is in Christ Jesus our Lord" (Rom 8:38–39).

Occasionally, adoptive families break under the stress of trying to parent children with enormous needs. Sometimes fathers and mothers give up, and a cycle of abandonment continues for the children. Human resources cannot heal some wounds. Families who are trying to parent children in severe crisis need the support of the church, and even more time spent thinking about God as their perfect Father. He is not intimidated by adopting older, special needs children—us! He will stay with us as we gradually receive the security, joy, and freedom he offers and as we try, as best we can, to pass that on as a heritage to our children.

While we are starting to learn how give to Benjamin a legacy of God's fatherly love, the Lord surprises us with a new twist on our journey. Our adoption agency tells us about severe flooding in the Mekong Delta of southern Vietnam. Orphanages are filled to overflowing with children who have lost their parents in the flood, and they ask all of their families to look for people who may be able to adopt some of these orphans. Benjamin has only been home for a few months, but we feel that we want one of those children. In the middle of our wait for Benjamin, when our emotional reserves were drained, it seemed improbable that we would start another adoption that might be just as difficult. But we pray about it, and now it seems like exactly what we should do. Our friends and family are surprised; we are rather surprised ourselves. But it seems natural and right. So we look to God, sharpen our pencils, and start filling out paperwork.

PART TWO—JOSIAH'S JOURNEY

Neither before nor after Josiah was there a king like him
Who turned to the Lord as he did—
With all his heart
And with all his soul
And with all his strength,
In accordance with all the Law of Moses

—2 Kings 23:25

INCARNATION

Our paperwork went quickly this time. We started in the summer and were finished by November, about a year after Benjamin's homecoming. With Benjamin we had no idea when the referral phone call was coming. But now we knew that our agency's facilitator was in Vietnam. She would take our family photo and information and translate it to the nuns who managed the orphanage, who would pray until they felt they knew which child was right for us. We were encouraged to think that prayer was a part of the match on both ends. We knew the facilitator's return date and that week were especially eager to pick up the phone.

The call came. We learned of a boy, born almost a year earlier, apparently healthy, in the orphanage and cleared for adoption. I hung up swirling with emotion. It was wonderful news. Yet I was disappointed. He was about to have his first birthday. I had been fondly imagining holding a small infant. We had heard that five-week old babies had recently been referred to families. Missing Benjamin's infancy had made me sensitive. I really wanted a baby, a little baby. I wanted to be there when he first laughed and walked and talked. Kathryn and Clara also wanted a tiny baby brother. Those at the orphanage and in our agency wanted to honor our request for a young infant, but apparently at that time there were no younger children legally ready for adoption. They wanted to be careful to give us a child with a simple background so that we would not get entrenched in another difficult delay.

I was distressed to realize the intensity of my expectations about this child's age. I reminded myself that God was putting our family together. He knows what is best for us. How could I make these self-centered demands? And how could I be so heartless, feeling particular about weeks and months when the life of this child is at risk? Besides, he is really still a baby, and will be even if it takes him several months to reach home. The difference between twelve weeks and twelve months is small in the whole context of his life. But my reasoning was slow in moving from mind to heart.

We did want this little boy. We asked our agency to pursue the adoption and scrambled to send necessary documentation before we left for Thanksgiving travel. We received the baby's photo and gazed at the face that stared out at us from the computer screen. We were charmed by his wide eyes and wispy hair, as he stood holding onto the bars of his crib. Yet my disappointment about his age remained.

As with Benjamin, we wondered whether we should celebrate our not-yet-adopted boy's first birthday. We decided to do something in his honor to tell him about later and invited a few friends for a party. I planned for all the children to draw pictures to hang above his crib and make predictions about the foods, toys, and songs he might like best on his next birthday.

Just before everyone was to arrive, I went out to buy balloons. Driving home, the back of the car was filled with festive balls of helium, and I was smitten with sadness. Why must we celebrate, again, a first birthday with the celebrant not present? Why must we miss his whole first year of life, that year that should be so vibrant and exciting and full of cherished milestones?

I wondered if my disappointment about his age revealed that I would also be upset if we discovered some major physical or emotional disabilities that could not be taken care of with a little time at home. Why do I expect to be able to set my own specifications like this? By choosing to adopt, we choose to enter a story of sorrow and loss, and we cannot expect to control everything. If we want to enter into this child's life, we need to do so without conditions that he will fit neatly into our plans.

It strikes me that this boy not being home for his first birthday is only one small part of a broader tragedy. He was conceived and born in such a place that his birth mother felt the need to leave him. He will probably never know her, his birth father, or his whole story. We will participate in mending what is broken but will not be able to restore those painful beginnings or fill in the missing parts of his life. Our losing this first year is only one manifestation of a little life begun with loss. I am sad for this baby.

Still driving home in the balloon-filled car, it strikes me that we are following in the footsteps of Jesus. My instinct is to move away from pain. But Jesus does not turn from our tragedies; he joins us in them, entering willingly into our messy lives. To walk with us, he left perfection and was born into the world, naked and cold. He spent years living and walking and talking with people shattered with grief and shame. He did not remove himself from earthly afflictions but chose to feel thirst, exhaustion, homelessness. He welcomed those who came to him for comfort and help, even when others thought he should send them away. He cried at the death of his friend. His heart went out to a widow whose only son had died. He decided to love and spend his life with a group of men he knew would betray, deny, and abandon him.

Jesus shows his willingness to enter our imperfect lives most powerfully by his death, when he bore all the pain from all of our sin. He went far beyond what any of us have suffered individually as he willingly took upon himself others' suffering and pain. He chooses to be near our grief.

Jesus suffered throughout his life, sharing in the kinds of pain we endure. He suffered on the cross the consequence of

our sins, a pain we have never known. He was described by
Isaiah as "a man of sorrows, and familiar with suffering. Like
one from whom men hide their faces he was despised, and
we esteemed him not. Surely he took up our infirmities and
carried our sorrows, yet we considered him stricken by God,
smitten by him, and afflicted" (Is 53: 3–4).

Isaiah said that the coming Savior would preach good
news for the poor, proclaim freedom for captives, bind up the
brokenhearted, and comfort all who mourn (Is 61:1–2). Early
in his public ministry, Jesus proclaimed that this Savior had
arrived (Lk 4:16–21). Ever since, he comforts us out of his
own real experience of sorrow—it is the most compassionate
nurse who tends our wounds. The cuts still hurt, the bandag-
ing hurts. But there is a sweetness in the pain, because of the
one who touches it. We are tended by a wounded healer.

Precious to me during these adoptions have become the
words of Hudson Taylor, the great 19th century missionary
to China: "Well, it is but a little while and He will appear to
answer all enigmas and to wipe away all tears. I would not
wish, then, to be of those who had none to wipe away, would
you?"[17] How I cherish the wiping away of my tears by Jesus.

Yes, it is sad that this child is in an impoverished orphanage in Vietnam. We know nothing about his birth parents and
would likely have our hearts pierced if we did. I think of other
adoptive families, bearing even heavier burdens of grief as
they parent children who have memories of abuse or other
severe physical or emotional wounds. But with Jesus near we
can bear sadness. In his presence the sadness can even become
sweet, because he does not stand aloof but enters in to weep
with us and dry our tears.

Jesus not only enters our sorrows, but he redeems them,
claims them for his good purposes, and transforms them. The
hurts may not be erased, but they can be taken into the Lord's
hand, and from the scars he may create something wonderful

for his kingdom. He will enter into these orphans' lives and reclaim the loss; perhaps we will be allowed to do it with him. What an immense privilege to follow him, ever so weakly.

What if I gave up my goals for a picture-perfect family with cooing baby in arms? What if I believed that I do not need to erase all the hurts? What if I entered this child's life, with Jesus, looked for how to apply his ointment to the wounds, then watched for him to create beauty from ashes? How freeing this could be.

We are following in the footsteps of the Man of Sorrows. I feel released from the anxiety about this child's beginnings, and I am willing to lose his infancy. I am sad for him but am more willing to live with that sadness, heartened to think that by choosing to enter a child's broken life we are choosing to follow Jesus. Home with balloons, I am able to celebrate the first birthday of a dear little boy. My dear little boy.

A BEAUTIFUL BABY

L ate on Christmas Eve, after the children are nestled all snug in their beds, we sit in front of the lighted tree and decide our new son's name. He will be Josiah Taylor. We are inspired by the biblical king Josiah, who loved God with all of his heart and brought the word of God to his people, and by Hudson Taylor, 19th century missionary to China and one of our favorite heroes. We are eager to bring this little Josiah home, and everything seems to be working smoothly toward that end.

Josiah's orphanage is in a different province than Benjamin's, and provincial rules require two adoptive parent visits, the first to present the application for adoption in person and the second to complete the adoption and bring the child home. We decide to send Phil alone for the first trip and go together for the second. So, early in January, Phil boarded a plane headed for Ho Chi Minh City, going to meet our new son and petition for his adoption.

Phil spent five days in Vietnam. He was able to visit Josiah for several hours each day. He also submitted his paperwork to the court and had time to get to know other adoptive parents. Their dynamic guide and interpreter escorted the parents to Viet Cong war tunnels and colorful restaurants. And Phil frequented the Internet café down the street from his hotel to write to us about his adventures.

At home, the children and I busied ourselves with school, social activities, and the stomach flu. And each day I hovered by the computer, poring over the e-mail updates from Phil. I read them over and over, relishing every detail:

I met Josiah. He had just woken up from a nap. He hung onto me pretty tightly. When they handed him to me, they pushed his little head and said the equivalent of 'Here's your papa' several times. He's a beautiful little baby. He has fair hair and big eyes and long eyelashes.

* * * * * *

We played for a long time with the photo set you made for him. I tried to show him all of you and tell him your names. He sits up by himself and stands by himself. He has delicate features. I took a lot of pictures. I really wish you could have been here. He fell asleep in my arms, slept for a little cat nap, and then woke up again. Then I took him to his room; he shares it with about twenty other kids. It'll be really hard to leave him here for another forty-five days.

* * * * * *

The big news of the day is that I went to court to present my application. 'May I see your passport please?' Oops. Left it at the front desk of the hotel. (They ask for it when you check in.) OK, let the other families go first. Ride with the driver back to the hotel. Get the passport and then go back to court. Get it processed. All seems to have gone through. We were given a date of 28 February.

* * * * * *

Just got back from a visit with Josiah. We played with the pictures. I gave presents to the workers. Josiah had a great time with Pat the Bunny and Ottie and Benjamin's dog. I also got him to walk. It looks like he just learned. He walked between me and an orphanage worker a few times. He looked pleased with himself. He's really comfortable around me. Smiled a lot when we were playing together.

* * * * * *

This is getting a little surreal. The facilitator, took us out to dinner tonight. He was talking about having snake blood. Since he was laughing when he said it, I thought he was kidding. We show up at the restaurant and lo and behold, you go by a zoo on the way to the table. First, there were the chicks and the doves. Below were the snakes. Then there were the monkeys and iguanas, then a sea turtle and bats.

* * * * * *

We sit down at the table. All of a sudden, this guy comes out with a live cobra! He lets it loose on the floor for everyone to see. The snake is trying to slither away, but the man has a long metal rod to pull the snake back. He picks it up by the tail and holds it at arm's length. After playing with the snake a while, he pins the head of the snake on the floor with the rod and grabs its tail and just behind its head. Then he takes some forceps and clamps the mouth shut. Then he drains the blood out of the snake. Then he chops the head off and the snake's body is still wiggling around. Then they served the drained blood mixed with whiskey. Fortunately, this is for the table next to us. But then he comes back with another snake—it's for our table. I bowed out of the snake blood and whiskey. Then, they put the still-beating heart of the snake on a little dish and James (one of the other adoptive dads) drinks it down with blood and whiskey. The guy comes out with the third snake for the other table next to us. The guest jumps out of his chair, because the snake was a bit too close. They then serve fried minced snake meat with

crushed peanuts, cold raw snake and onions, and snake soup.
Oh, and there was a side of french fries. No ketchup.

* * * * * *

The cobra event elicited many chuckles from us at home.
And there was a deeper undercurrent to my smiles as I shared
the story, because I knew that this week was very significant
to Phil. His trip to Vietnam just over a year earlier had triggered a crisis in his faith. Phil had struggled to reconcile the
things he had seen in Vietnam with what he believed about
God. After some twists and turns, his crisis led him to delve
into the lasting effects of his experiences growing up with
racial bullying. He discovered connections between his childhood traumas and his adult reactions to people and to risk-
taking.

After a year of this emotional work, the Lord sent Phil
back to Vietnam for a field trip. His counselor was excited
about this trip and encouraged Phil to take prudent risks, to
adventurously put himself into uncomfortable situations and
enjoy the experience of seeing God care for him. It was an
opportunity for Phil to be alone in a place that had been
difficult for him and to replace fear and suspicion with trust,
enjoyment, and freedom. Phil wrote from the Internet café
of his prudent risks: walking down small alleys by himself,
and eating iced mango, which guide books warn may harbor
nasty micro-organisms.

But who would have imagined that Phil's risk-taking
would have included sitting among live cobras (cornered at a
table that backed onto a river, no less), then, as he relayed in
the rest of that e-mail letter, riding back to the hotel through
crowded Ho Chi Minh City by a driver who had consumed
too much beer? It was a dramatic field trip indeed.

Our trips for Josiah came at a rocky time in Vietnamese adoptions. There were hints of babies being illegally sold;
one facilitator had left the country and was being investigated.
Fraudulent agencies doing adoptions in Vietnam were being
exposed and shut down. We were relieved that most of these
cases seem to have been in independent adoptions, that our
agency watched out for ethically shady situations and always
worked through reputable orphanages. But sometimes there
are dark doings in international adoption, as in all other parts
of a corrupted world, and we learned about some of these just
before Phil left. If he was going to be at peace in Vietnam, it
would not be by deciding that his perception of evil and suffering was unfounded, but because he was entrusting himself
to the Lord in the midst of it.

And Phil, feeling all his weakness on this trip, certainly
did not go expecting he would be able to encourage faith
in others he met. One father was suffering to the point of
breakdown from the stress of his adoption. Since Phil had
been similarly shaken just a year earlier, he was able to em-
pathize and pray for him. Others' deep needs surfaced, and
Phil was able to encourage them. I still smile to think of the
gentle, timely, and sometimes even humorous ways that God
arranged the details of this trip.

Phil's verses for meditation that week were about darkness and light: "Even in darkness light dawns for the upright,
for the gracious and compassionate and righteous man." (Ps
112:4); "I will lead the blind by ways they have not known,
along unfamiliar paths I will guide them; I will turn the
darkness into light before them and make the rough places
smooth." (Is 42:16)

In the Old Testament, light is used as a picture of God's
guidance and blessing to his people. Later, Jesus announced:
"I have come into the world as a light, so that no one who
believes in me should stay in darkness … I am the light of the

world. Whoever follows me will never walk in darkness, but will have the light of life" (Jn 8:12; 12:46). Phil's experience during this significant journey was of darkness changed into light, a light that spilled onto others.

We received Phil back home with great joy. We pored over photos of Josiah, which I carried everywhere—I showed pictures of my adorable little boy to anyone who would look. Now we eagerly prepared for the day, only about a month away, when we would go back to Vietnam to bring Josiah into our family.

DELAY

The paperwork for Josiah is moving along smoothly. We are scheduled to leave on February 25 and legally adopt him on February 28. I have spent hours on the phone figuring out the complicated sets of flights. The families that Phil met on his trip all have the same court date; we are sending travel itineraries to each other, and Phil is looking forward to introducing me to them. About three weeks before we are to travel, my excitement surfaces. Earlier, perhaps not really believing it could be happening so soon, I had been reserved. But now, thrilled anticipation starts to stream out of the cracks in my dike.

Then comes the phone call. Our Hope's Promise social worker, Jennifer, who had waited helplessly with us through long months with Benjamin, has news she does not want to share.

There is a problem with Josiah's paperwork. Apparently when the hospital sent the report to the court, it was for a different baby. They are working on straightening out the confusion and will inform us of our new court date when it is resolved. The facilitator in Vietnam is hopeful that it will not be too long, maybe only several weeks. It seems to just be clerical error. But no one knows when we will be told to travel, and there is apparently nothing we can do to expedite it.

This news knocks me down. I do not feel I can face another fight of faith. A several-week wait does not seem so bad, but the indefinites make it feel unbearable. Maybe we were given information for the wrong child; maybe all his paperwork has always been wrong and will have to be started over. Maybe, as we suspected with Benjamin's delay, there is another issue that the authorities in Vietnam are concealing.

I have to tell Phil and our children this bad news, and again try to encourage them to trust God when I am terribly shaken myself. Once more we have to change our plans (more hours on the phone, this time canceling the flights). We were so eager to embrace Josiah and carry him home, and it is devastating to think we may be be apart from him for weeks or months longer. Again a hope about to be realized is yanked away, like a rug from under our feet, leaving us reeling.

Several times while waiting for Benjamin we thought we would travel soon, and were then strung along to another unexplained delay. Now my emotional memory reacts. It is like when 2-year-old Kathryn, after a hospitalization involving many prods and needles, recoiled from anyone in a white jacket. I do not feel strong enough to engage in another time of intense prayer and waiting. I do not want to pull our friends and family into another such time either, yet I keenly feel the need for their prayer.

Waves of temptation bear down on me as I start to live with this delay. I see a choice before me about whether I will stand in confident trust or be controlled by a sense of dread. I have opportunity to lay hold of the faith that has been given to me, faith that was forged during the trial of waiting for Benjamin, but that now feels frail. I do not want to settle into a grim, resigned determination; I want to testify instead that I know the joy of the Lord in the midst of this painful development and unknown future.

The weeks after this development are uncertain. Should I agree to play in that concert in April? Do we plan to attend the family reunion in June? We try to keep our calendars flexible yet cannot put our whole life on hold when we may not get Josiah for a long time. We call the adoption agency once a week, knowing they will tell us when they learn anything, yet feeling an almost desperate need to keep asking.

I see my poverty of spirit three weeks after the news of the delay, during the week we had been scheduled to adopt Josiah. I realize that I feel bitter towards the Lord, feeling that he is treating us unjustly and unkindly. We went through so much getting Benjamin home. Why does it have to be our case that is scrambled? I try to be happy for the families who are on the eve of adopting their children, but I realize the weak and self-centered state of my heart. At times I do not even care about growing in faith through this opportunity. I do not want to be joyful in affliction, as I think the Lord is challenging. I just want what I want, like a spoiled child. With the riches of church and husband and three beautiful children, I am miserable because I can not have the fourth when I thought I could, miserable because God will not reveal to me what the future holds or assure me that Josiah's adoption will have a happy ending.

My love for the Lord is feeble. I recognize this, and it reminds me that Jesus was crucified so that he could bring me, self-centered and impoverished as I am, to be with him. When my raging frustration and fear settle down enough for me to listen, the Lord challenges me through the third chapter of Philippians:

" ... But whatever was to my profit I now consider loss for the sake of Christ. What is more, I consider everything a loss compared to the surpassing greatness of knowing Christ Jesus my Lord, for whose sake I have lost all things" (Phil 3:7-8). Am I willing to loosen my grip on the hopes and dreams I have for Josiah and my family? Do I consider those dreams nothing when compared to knowing Christ? Will I gladly, quietly look to him and open myself to his fellowship, even if I do not understand what he is doing? Do I value my relationship with him more than anything?

" ... I count them rubbish that I may gain Christ and be found in him..." (Phil 3:8–9). Is getting Josiah home comparative rubbish when set next to the treasure of knowing Christ? If I put my most cherished family and personal dreams up next to knowing God, which has a stronger draw? Can I say that I want to know Christ more than I want any of his gifts?

"... not having a righteousness of my own that comes from the law, but that which is through faith in Christ—the righteousness that comes from God and is by faith" (Phil:9). The answer to my questions is no: I do not always cherish Jesus more than his gifts. I don't hold so lightly onto everything else that I can call it rubbish. My faith is weak and my devotion to God is low. A piece of bad news sends me spiraling into fear and doubt. I am ashamed about this. Yet here is my salvation. He gives me his own righteousness. Christ claims me, and he will change me. This will be my hope today, for the rest of my life, and when I stand before my judge.

" ... I want to know Christ and the power of his resurrection and the fellowship of sharing in his sufferings, becoming like him in his death, and so, somehow, to attain to the resurrection from the dead" (Phil:11). Here are words to make me cringe. Must knowing Jesus involve sharing in his suffering? Loving God and loving people includes suffering. I need faith to believe that the fellowship with him includes treasures that outweigh the pain. Will this adoption of Josiah include fellowship with Jesus in the form of suffering? I pray that he will strengthen me to face this possibility.

I have recognized the weakness in my faith and love for God. My hardhearted bitterness is replaced by a repentant and quiet heart that knows its pervasive weakness but also knows where to go to be restored. I cry out, again, with the desperate father of the demon-possessed boy, "Oh Lord, I do believe.

Help me in my unbelief." I am willing to live in another time of uncertainty and vulnerability, if only I can cling to Jesus.

On the afternoon of February 28, the day we had thought we would be officially adopting Josiah, I pull into the driveway and see beautiful flowers sitting on the porch. I walk up to them, children trailing at my heels. The flowers are from our small-group Bible study and the card reads that they are standing with us on behalf of Josiah, with faith that God is working all things together for good.

Together we are invited, again, to a time of faith in the unseen. My children wonderingly watch me hold the flowers and cry, sweet tears, not bitter, but thankful and weak and loved.

ANOTHER TREASURE IN OUR ARMS

Lift up your eyes and look about you:
All assemble and come to you:
Your sons come from afar,
And your daughters are carried on the arm.
Then you will look and be radiant,
Your heart will throb and swell with joy.
Your sun will never set again,
And your moon will wane no more;
The Lord will be your everlasting light,
And your days of sorrow will end.

—Isaiah 60:3-4

The call came, this time with good news. We were cleared to adopt Josiah. Jennifer from Hope's Promise left messages for me at home and for Phil at work; we discovered them and frantically called each other. Glorious words like those above rang in my heart during the two weeks before we traveled. The redemption promised in Isaiah has not yet completely arrived, but it has started. The glory of the Lord has come to us in Jesus. One son has already come from afar, and the second is coming. In this victory we see the beginning of what God will someday finish for the entire cosmos.

"This is about redemption," I declared as we scrambled to get ready for the trip. God was going to lift Josiah out of the darkness of being an orphan and set him into the light of being part of a family and church, out of poverty and into wealth—not just material wealth, but the multifaceted wealth of home and community, of promises and resources and commitment and love. It felt like a glorious deliverance. God loves to rescue people. We see it graphically in this orphan-to-son redemption.

After a flurry of logistics and then weighty goodbyes with our three children, we retraced our path from Michigan to Ho Chi Minh City. The tone of Phil's earlier trip to meet Josiah continued as we went together to adopt him. We rejoiced in the visible tokens of God's presence in this place.

Several hours after we arrived in Vietnam, after again being whisked off to the hotel and then told we would be taken to our baby, we found ourselves on a long porch outside rooms full of babies and children in a rural Vietnamese orphanage. An orphanage worker delivered a boy into our arms, and we physically became parents to another child. I wrote to Kathryn, Clara, and Benjamin as soon as we could get to a computer that evening:

> They had us sit down to wait and went to get Josiah. I didn't want to wait! My heart was going fast. They woke him up from his nap, then brought him to us in a few minutes. He was sleepy and serious looking, but went right to Papa without crying. And then after a few minutes he came to me, too. He seems to like to snuggle. He is a beautiful, sweet baby. You will love him. He was pretty serious (like Benjamin was at first), but he hardly cried at all. He just looked around with his big eyes and held on to us. He's got incredibly long eyelashes and pudgy cheeks and legs. He likes to suck his thumb and put things in his mouth. He raises his eyebrows. He's still pretty wobbly on his feet. We love looking at him. Can't wait for you to meet him.

At the orphanage, we had several minutes to spend alone with Josiah. Then we were taken to a large room where about twenty young children were milling around. There was not much furniture; it was apparently just a gathering place. The one or two workers there did not pay much attention to us, as we stood with our new toddler son. So we played. We read *Pat the Bunny*; several small children drew near to Phil to listen. We emptied the Cheerios we had brought for Josiah into many appreciative small hands. Then, the contents of our diaper bag having been exhausted, we started to sing. We were happy to discover that enjoyment of much of our repertoire of toddler tunes was not dependent on familiarity with English. Attentive, giggling children surrounded us, trying to imitate "Head, Shoulders, Knees, and Toes" and every other boisterous song we could think of. How they relished the attention. How we enjoyed their beautiful, uplifted faces. I wanted to remember these precious little people, made in God's image and yearning for relationships.

At the end of that afternoon in the orphanage, we were able to take Josiah with us to the hotel. We kept him with us every minute of the rest of the trip. Josiah was most assuredly the son of our hearts. We gazed at him. We delighted in each smile that broke out on his little face, each little sound he made, each new food he learned how to eat, each transition that he successfully passed through. We overflowed with thankfulness for his safe delivery to us. He was a warm, bright manifestation of God's light.

There was brightness in other relationships during this trip, as well. We arrived in Ho Chi Minh City at the same time as another adoptive family, a mother and 15-year-old son, who were there to adopt little Rebecca while father and other siblings waited at home. We went with them to the orphanage and courts and U.S. Consulate, discovered new restaurants, swapped tips on how to use the computers at the Internet café, watched the daily changes in each others' children. Several days later another family came, then two more. One of the couples was coming to adopt a 2-year-old boy from Josiah's orphanage. Phil had enjoyed playing with this boy the day we picked up Josiah and had looked at him sadly when it was time for us to leave, thinking: "You need a dad."

We did not know that his new dad was then preparing to
fly to Vietnam to claim him. How glad we were to see these
other children welcomed into families!

When we started our first adoption, we did not know
many adoptive families. We would have been reassured to
have someone going with us on the same path. On our trip
to pick up Benjamin, we met only one other adoptive mother
briefly before we left. Now, here they were, other families like
us, thrown together in Ho Chi Minh City at a time of momentous family transition. They, like us, had experienced the
strain of waiting and were feeling the same tender concern
for their newly grafting children. It warmed our hearts and
gave the trip a celebratory feel.

We were even able to worship with others on this trip. It
is not simple to find a gathering of Sunday Christian worship
in Ho Chi Minh City. We had tried but not succeeded on the
first trip; neither had Phil for his trip alone. This time we had
the name of a hotel that we were told hosted an international
fellowship. We hoped it was similar to what we enjoyed during our year in Shanghai, a small group of people from all
over the world (except for China, whose government did not
allow them to participate), worshipping together in the midst
of their overseas experience.

Two of the other families came with us to try to find this
fellowship. We stepped out of the heat into the cool opulence
of the hotel and followed signs to the second floor. Walking
out of the elevator, we heard instruments warming up before
the service. Tears welled in my eyes, as they did during the
next two hours. There was power in the worship of these
men, women, and children from all over Europe and Asia
(except for Vietnam, whose government did not allow them
to participate). The presence of the Lord was like the brightness of a beam in a dark room, not dimmed by other light.
"Hail Jesus, He's My King" was a joyful but sober pledge of

allegiance. All the songs were weighty with meaning. The affirmation of God's power was more meaningful, the songs of commitment more serious, because of their proclamation in the midst of a country whose government represses many of its people, including those who profess faith in Christ.

During that morning, people spoke of a movement of prayer for Ho Chi Minh City. They intended to come together to pray for the city, hoping that God would stretch out his hand to bind up Vietnam's wounds. I had wanted to pray for Vietnam since we started our first adoption, and especially since our trip for Benjamin. My prayers often faltered, but in this week I tasted their fruit. God has called others to love and intercede for the people of Vietnam. On our first trip, we experienced God's faithfulness to our boys and our family. This time, he let us see some of what he is doing to mend the brokenness that brought these boys to our family.

On our first trip, our joy at having Benjamin was great but shadowed by tension. Phil was hurt by the poverty he saw around him; I did not understand the depths of his angst. I wanted to explore the city during our days of waiting for paperwork; he wanted to stay in the hotel. I was nervous about how the family would adjust when we returned home. Each with our own stress, we did not always know how to care for each other.

This time, I suggested staying at the hotel some days to rest; he thought about what outings we could undertake. We laughed together at the colorful adventures of overseas travel. We enjoyed trying different restaurants, one of which piped Christmas music out of its speakers. We relished the experience of eating noodles and drinking mango nectar while looking out of the window at the steaming hot street teeming with motorbikes and pedestrians—and listening to "Winter Wonderland" and "White Christmas."

We were even able to enjoy an unexpected visit to a Vietnamese hospital. During Josiah's physical (required for a U.S. visa), the doctor heard a heart murmur. We were immediately whisked off to a cardiac hospital for evaluation. We did not know exactly what was happening but were concerned when told that Josiah would undergo a procedure and would need to be sedated if he cried. We prayed. His health and his visa might be at risk. But we also enjoyed watching the activities of a Vietnamese hospital. We sat on benches waiting our turn and were then squeezed into a corner of a small room where a man was given a cardiac ultrasound while the elderly doctor taught the thirteen students crushed behind him.

When it was Josiah's turn, we fed a steady stream of pretzels into his mouth to stave off any crying. And we had a limited but lovely chat with the gracious doctor, who looked at Josiah's ultrasound, proclaimed cheerfully, "No sweat," and then asked us if Americans still said "no sweat," a phrase he had picked up from soldiers during the war. We were bemused at this warm-hearted doctor's interactions with the students, wondering what he was telling them to make them smile and laugh. God gave us grace to enjoy this hospital visit, even though it might have turned into a delay or problem with the adoption.

Throughout the trip, we were assured that the Lord was caring for us and working in Vietnam. It encouraged us to continue praying for the country, and it freed us to enjoy the time we spent there.

But also throughout the intensity of these ten days, during the delightful time with Josiah, while enjoying the exploration and worship and new friends, we dearly missed our other children. We longed to have the whole family united under the home roof. So our hearts sang when the paperwork sped through, when we learned the trip would be three days shorter than Benjamin's, and when we successfully changed our flights home. With all of this—just a little taste of God's ultimate redemption—we were radiant. We were ready to carry our son home from afar.

WATCH THEM SLEEP

Over the Pacific on the way home with Josiah, the plane is quiet except for the steady engine hum. A few small television screens flicker blue light onto passengers who blankly stare at cooking shows, movies, or the ever-changing statistics of altitude and outdoor temperature and miles to destination. Most are trying to sleep. Josiah, after hours of squirming and dropping food and toys onto the floor, has finally fallen asleep. A kind flight attendant has moved us into a row that is not quite full so that Josiah can lie across my lap with feet dangling into the next seat.

I want this travel-weary baby to sleep and am afraid to move a muscle lest I wake him. Because of his head nestled in my arm, I do not attempt to read or talk or even push the television monitor button. I find I cannot sleep with such restricted movement. So there is nothing for me to do for an hour or two but look at him, think, and pray.

It is a sweet time. I cherish being able to study Josiah's face. I marvel at how wonderfully it has been formed—how beautiful are his long eyelashes and delicately chiseled ears. I wonder if his birth mother was ever able to gaze at that face and marvel at it, or if her life was so full of crisis and pain and fear that she could not stop to reflect on the miracle of a perfectly made baby.

This little person now nestled in my arm has a life ahead of him and an eternal soul. He has relationships and joys and sorrows waiting in the wings that will go into him and form the person he becomes. He will love and be loved, influence and be influenced. And I will have the immense honor of playing a large part in the growth of his body and soul. My life and his will be intimately connected for eternity. I am awed at the privilege of being a mother.

I wonder again about his birth mother. Does she ever think about him? Though we know nothing about her, it is likely that she is extremely impoverished, that her leaving him at the hospital was an act of desperation caused by circumstances I cannot fathom. What happens to the relationship with a child born to you when you have to leave him, or her? Do you remember your baby often, and does the memory give you joy, or pain, or blankness? Is your life so full of immediate and tangible needs that it forces out time to muse on the beautiful face of your newborn baby, to wonder about where he is and who knows and loves him? I do not presume to understand. I do not know Josiah's birth mother and have never had her experience.

However, I realize in this moment that I do not often study and marvel at my own children's faces. I do not often remember the wonder it is to live with eternal souls. I do not often feel in awe of the enormous privilege of having connection with those souls, connection that will, Lord willing, last forever.

My daily stressors are much less potent than those of Josiah's birthmother. Spilled milk, toilet training accidents, whiny voices, unfinished phone calls, sibling bickers, piles of paperwork. These can wear me down bit by bit until my body is tense and my mind frazzled. Days full of these relentless small annoyances push out perspective-broadening times of gazing at marvelous little faces. What do I do at home that has the same effect on me as this motionless holding of my sleeping child? Very little. I am aware of the precious gift of this hour.

Many of the psalms must have come out of such quiet reflective time. Perhaps walking for miles to your destination provided the same kind of space as flying suspended between continents. God broadened people's vision when they were unharried and listening. He showed them his majesty. He reminded them of his past work on their behalf and built their storehouse of faith for the future: "I remember the days of long ago; I meditate on all your works and consider what your hands have done" (Ps143:5).

Many other psalms plead for help in times of crisis. They cry out to God when facing danger from enemies within and enemies without. Some of these (Psalm 120, for example) seem to end abruptly, the writer still in emotional turmoil, not having reached a place of praise and peace. But other psalms start from a position of fear or anger and end in worshipful meditation about God's greatness and goodness, his strength and justice and care. The time of reflection lifts the writer above the swarming crises and allows him to see them with transformed perspective. Then and now, our lives have a rhythm of agitation changing into peace. In the midst of earthquakes and crumbling mountains and nations in uproar God says to us: "Be still and know that I am God; I will be exalted among the nations, I will be exalted in the earth" (Ps 46:10).

Men and women of ancient times, without cars or computers, airplanes or stock markets, experienced the same emotions and life dynamics as we do. It is a happy thought that their souls were fed in the same ways that ours can be, and that we can be encouraged in our reflections by theirs.

As I sit still and silent in the dark plane, I realize how much I need this unrushed time. I want to hold onto this wonder and joy and not be swept off for days by small frustrations. I want to cherish my relationships with these children, live life richly with them, inspire them. I want praise and wonder and joy to spill out to them from me. This will only happen, I think, if I am often still and quiet. There will always be unfinished work demanding my attention. But let me remember this time cradling Josiah on the plane. Let me remember the joy of being lifted out of the immediate and set into the broad, wondrous picture of the presence of eternity in my children and work. Let me remember that perhaps the best I can do for my children is to watch them while they sleep.

ORPHAN TO SON

I will not leave you as orphans; I will come to you.
—Jesus Christ (Jn 14:18)

I have beheld the beauty of two orphans transforming into sons. During the months of waiting for Benjamin, we periodically received photos. In every picture he looked heavy and serious, never smiling. I put them next to photos from his very first days at home, where he is grinning, laughing, radiant—the contrast is dramatic. He must have sometimes smiled at the orphanage, and he certainly has had miserable moments at home. But the overall transformation captured in the photos is striking; and a beautiful picture of what has happened in his life.

Our two sons were similar in their adjustments to a family. When first taken from the orphanage, they were stoic—alert and serious, yet not tearful. During the first days with us at the hotel, they slowly shed their defensive seriousness and revealed smiles and tentative play. However, when we left the hotel room and ventured out into the swirling streets they became visibly alarmed. For several days both Benjamin and Josiah yelped or cried at any point of transition—when entering or exiting taxis, leaving the hotel, or coming back in. They cried more if we did not hold them constantly. This made it an exhausting challenge to eat in restaurants, sign official papers, shop, or sightsee. I wrote home from the Internet café with flying fingers, hearing Josiah's cries break through the street noise as Phil walked him back and forth on the pavement outside.

Benjamin and Josiah's reactions were understandable. Before we came, they had rarely left the confines of their or-

phanage rooms. Now they were whisked off to different places every day. Their senses were overloaded with sights, sounds,
and smells they had never experienced. The people caring for
them looked and sounded entirely different from anyone they
had ever known.

We so wanted our boys to know that they were safe, that
something good was happening to them. We wanted to communicate that we would take care of them, that they did not
need to fear all these new things. But we could not. Even if
we could have spoken to them in Vietnamese, they could not
have understood that all we were doing was for their good.
They could not comprehend that when we frightened them
by going in and out of hotel and taxi we were doing the work
that made them legally our sons and that would allow them
to travel to their new home.

We hurt for the boys, but we could not shield them from
all fearful transitions. We had to leave the relative quiet of
the hotel at times and enter the fray; besides, we hoped that
these temporary changes would prepare them for the big trip
that was coming. Through these daily outings, they gradually
learned that we would always be there to feed them, hold
them, and wipe their tears. Then, we hoped, they would feel
more secure when we flew to the other side of the world,
where the sights and sounds and smells were *really* different.

Those days of stress in Ho Chi Minh City were worth the
tears. After Josiah had been with us for nine days, we returned
to his orphanage to say goodbye. The women who had cared
for him smiled and put out their arms to hold him, but he
clung to Phil. For the caretakers' sakes, I would have been glad
for Josiah to show more affection, but I was very thankful that
he felt safe in his Papa's arms.

In their first weeks at home, both Benjamin and Josiah
seemed to adapt remarkably well to their new home and family. They seemed to thrive so well that at times it looked as

though a bit of jet lag would be their hardest adjustment.

But behaviors occasionally surfaced that reminded us of the boys' fearful reactions those first days in Vietnam. I called them orphan remnants. Both Benjamin and Josiah felt comfortable at home with their parents and sisters. But when others came or went they became visibly agitated and confused. At times, they would look around to take attendance of everyone in their family, checking that all were present. Benjamin preferred the whole family to be in the same room. And both boys were very upset when, after several days at home with us, Phil had to return to work. Morning after morning, Benjamin wailed as he watched Phil walk out the door.

Again we sympathized with them. The changes in their lives were enormous. How was Josiah to know that these two parents, two sisters, and brother would remain constant while others came and went? How could Benjamin understand that his father was not leaving permanently but would walk back through the same door in about ten hours? So many changes had just raged through their lives—how would they know that there were not more coming? There was nothing we could do but continue to be present for them until they felt secure. I wanted to be able to speak directly into their souls to alleviate their angst: "Stop acting like an orphan," I pled with Josiah (knowing he couldn't understand) "You're not an orphan anymore; you're our son!"

The legal declaration of a child's status usually comes in black and white: With signatures on paper and the ruling of a judge, a child changes from being a ward of the state to being the son or daughter of parents. But other changes from orphan to son or daughter spread through a child's life more gradually. It takes orphans *time* to live fully in their new identity. It takes *time*, when you have been an orphan, to believe you are a son. Pockets of orphan remnants may remain hidden for years and then surface unexpectedly. A complete, transforming adoption is gradual, and adoptive parents need perseverance when their children's deep hurts are not erased overnight.

Children should be cared for by adults who love them. A break in that care can lodge deep in their hearts and memories. We are thankful that Benjamin and Josiah received shelter, food, and some human interaction during their orphan chapter of life. Even so, they have known loss, and they still carry some orphan remnants that can prevent them from fully enjoying the love and safety of a family. Many children in the world live as true orphans, with all the aloneness and lack of protection that word connotes. The most deprived have to take care of themselves, developing survival skills and coping mechanisms, some of which horrify us. We have been shocked by video footage of children in Romanian orphanages who bang their heads against the walls repeatedly in order to compensate for lack of stimulation and human contact. Some of these children, when adopted by loving families, can never have secure attachments to others. Many Latin American children are thrown out of their abusive homes to live on their own in the streets. They grasp for menial jobs or beg or steal, and they sniff glue or paint solvent to dull their pain. Some of them, after years of fending for themselves, find it impossible to trust others who would love and help them. Families in Thailand and Cambodia sometimes sell their girls into prostitution. Most of these girls never return to their families and villages, or even to mainstream society, but live in the brothels with fear and shame, often dying young.

As I think about the coping behavior of abandoned orphans, and observe my own boys struggle to understand what it means to live in a family, I also think about my own life. As God's adopted daughter, I too, am being gradually transformed, as my behavior and emotions come to more closely match my real identity. My own hidden orphan remnants surface at times. Thinking about how orphans change into sons and daughters provides good opportunity for me to think about how I live in my spiritual adoptive family.

The day I had hoped to write this chapter, I woke up ill and then discovered a flooded basement. Phil had to leave, so I spent the day feeling sick, dragging soggy cardboard upstairs, and caring for four young children. They were not inclined to help me (in spite of the initial rush of excitement in having a wet basement), but they did seem partial to bickering with each other. I ran upstairs often to stop fights and to help Josiah with his new toilet skills. While throwing out dripping dust balls, I learned that the childcare I had hoped for was not coming. My day continued to go badly and I felt alone and resentful—like an orphan. I did not trust in my Father's care for me but acted as if I were left on my own to deal with problems. Since this chapter was simmering in my mind, I recognized my orphan feelings and turned back to my Father, who of course had been there with me the whole time.

Do I feel that I have been left on my own, that I need to manipulate situations to get what I need? "I will not leave you as orphans; I will come to you," says Jesus. Sons and daughters of God are not alone, nor will they ever be. Secure children of God know that their Father is with them. So they do not resent surprises that surface in a day, or feel flustered or fearful when whisked from one new place to another. They know they are well cared for, and so are released to enjoy life and to serve others.

Midway through our trip to adopt Benjamin, we visited a large hotel. Phil walked around the lobby with Benjamin while I browsed in a gift shop. I glanced up through the glass wall of the shop and saw Benjamin in Phil's arms. Benjamin made eye contact with me—and grinned. He was smiling for me. He was glad because he knew me. I was thrilled.

One evening shortly after that Benjamin played peek-a-boo with the elderly gentleman at a nearby table. He smiled and giggled. I was delighted again, because he had shed some of his suspicion and fear and was acting carefree and playful, as a nearly two-year-old boy should.

Orphans transformed into sons and daughters delight the hearts of their parents. I was sad for my sons when they showed their orphan remnants and delighted when they began relaxing and feeling secure. I reveled in their happiness. I loved to see Benjamin and Josiah play freely, to hear them laugh and watch them respond to my love with happiness and affection.

Does our Father delight in our happiness like this? He must be honored when our freedom and joy show that we trust his care for us. I am not an abandoned orphan, but a beloved child of God. But sometimes I forget. And he tells me: "Stop acting like an orphan; you are my daughter." I believe that he will gradually lead us all to live fully in our true identity—not as orphans, but as cherished sons and daughters.

IN HONOR OF THE ORPHANS

These things are not easy to look at for long. We turn away with burning eyes, and only for the children's sake could we ever look again.[18]

—Amy Carmichael

I look at my sons build block castles, run in the park, sleep in their beds. I watch chocolate ice cream dribble down their chins and I listen to them pray at the dinner table. And once in a while I think about where they might have been had we not adopted them. I am immensely thankful to see them safe and happy. I also remember the other children, those without blocks, parks, beds, ice cream, or families.

There may be about 30 million orphaned children around the world, defining orphan strictly as a child whose parents both have died. Broadening the definition to include children whose parents are unable or unwilling to care for them, the number becomes 70 million.[19] These are very rough estimates, since vulnerable children cannot stand up to be counted. Many of them are hidden, and many are suffering.

But even if we had precise numbers, most of these children would be abstract and faceless to us. Let us read the true stories of four children, in honor of all the others in crisis around the world, the hidden children whose lives have not been recorded by human pen.

Makara was an orphan living with her aunt in Cambodia when she was sold into slavery for about $200. She was taken to a dilapidated shack near Phnom Penh and forced into prostitution. Girls like Makara are usually taken far away from their homes so that they do not run away. They are dressed up and forced to attract and please clients, or face beatings. They cannot leave until they pay off their debt to the brokers who bought them, which is often impossible. If the girls ever do earn enough to escape the brothel, they are considered tarnished and thus are usually unable to return to their homes or start another life.

Makara is ill with some kind of systemic infection. She is barely able to speak above a whisper to the female physician who is trying to help her, terrified to answer even simple questions. The doctor says that she has probably suffered disease for a long time in silence, and that her timid manner indicates how unsafe she feels.

UNICEF estimates that one million children are forced into the multibillion dollar commercial sex trade every year.[20]

Nelson lives in Guatemala City, Guatemala. He ran away from home because his parents beat him. Now he lives on the streets with other boys, trying to find food and shelter and avoid abuse from the public and police. Many Guatemalans either loathe or are indifferent to these children.

Nelson admits that he steals to survive, usually managing to grasp enough for a few hamburgers or hot dogs every day. Like most of the thousands of street kids in Guatemala City, he is addicted to paint solvent, which dulls the hunger and cold.[21]

Millions of children live on the streets of Latin America's densely populated cities.

In a southern region of Rwanda are five brothers and sisters living in a mud hut. Tutsi soldiers killed their parents and older siblings, hacking them to pieces while the younger children fled. The soldiers chased Theresie, age 14, and sliced her left ear in half with a machete.

Theresie acts as mother to her three younger sisters, gathering wood and water and doing most of the housework and childcare. Food is scarce.

She starts crying when someone suggests that all this family responsibility must make her feel like a mother. "'I'm still young--I'm not like a mother,' she says through tears. 'I hope my sisters' future will be better than mine. I don't care about my own future...' She doesn't want to get married or start her own family. Her only dream can never be filled by any friend, neighbor or benevolent aid group. She weeps when asked what that is. 'I wish I could have parents like other children,' she says in anguish."

It is predicted that in several African countries at least one in five children will be orphaned (by war and AIDS) by 2010.[22]

Not all hurting children are overseas. Some, like Cari, are right here in the United States. For most of her childhood, Cari went back and forth from foster homes to her drug-addicted birth mother. She and her social worker once tried to count the number of foster homes she had lived in during her childhood; they stopped at fifty.

Cari's mother let men molest Cari; sometimes her mother was even in the same room, high on drugs, while Cari begged her to make them stop. She was also abused in some of her foster homes. She remembers being locked in a basement to sleep, and being given a small bag of sugar as her only food for three days. She says her worst memory is becoming pregnant by one of her foster parent's boyfriends when she was twelve years old. She released the baby girl to an adoptive home. Cari says: "Most people agree that children should be protected, but I don't think there was ever anyone there to protect me. I don't remember ever hearing the words 'I love you' as a child. I don't remember ever being hugged without motive."

Cari's mother's parental rights were terminated when she was thirteen, past the age when most families will consider adopting a child. She reached eighteen, left the foster care system, and was sent out on her own. She hoped that life would get better. But "I didn't care what happened to me. I would go to bed at night wishing I would just go to sleep and not wake back up. I felt like my life was worthless and it wouldn't matter if I was dead."

Cari met some Christians in high school who told her to pray. She always wanted a mom, and prayed for years that her birth mother would be there for her. Several years after she left foster care, God brought Cari to a church where people started to love her and help her make sense of her life. When she was twenty-six years old, she told one of them that God didn't answer prayers; she had prayed for a mom and he had not responded. He responded that maybe the prayer had been answered, but she was looking in the wrong direction. A couple weeks later, he and his wife told her that they wanted to adopt her. She thought they were joking. They talked and prayed and listened to her fears and questions--and they adopted her. "I didn't actually believe them until we got the papers signed from the judge. Even now, I still sometimes get scared that they will change their mind. I guess that's from being disappointed so many times before...Sometimes, I'm still sad at all that I feel that I've missed out on. But, I'm very grateful that I do now have a family of my own."

There are 500,000 children in the U.S. foster care system; 135,000 of them are available for adoption.[23]

Jesus told his disciples to not hinder the children from coming to him. He took children in his arms, put his hands on them and blessed them. (Mark 10:14, 16). Why are some orphans led into the arms of Jesus and others left outside? I do not know, and it pains me to write about the new life of our two sons while thinking about these others. But Cari's story announces that there can be hope for these orphans, and at least in part through God's people--Cari's adoptive father is one of the pastors at her church.

Orphans at home and around the world can share our rich inheritance. They can run into the arms of Jesus and be transformed from orphans into sons and daughters. We are not all called to adopt these children into our families. But we are all called to look at them, even though it makes our eyes burn, and be willing to let their needs disrupt our lives. Let us not hesitate because of inconvenience, difficulty, or fear. God will meet and bless us as we love the children in his name.

CHILDREN OF THE HEAVENLY FATHER

Of all the children I know, Josiah most relishes his times of sleep. Other toddlers in my acquaintance, when asked if they would like to take a nap or told that it's bedtime, shake their heads vigorously or protest. Sometimes Josiah does that too, but more often he gives a slow nod while inserting his thumb in his mouth. He and I both savor our pre-sleep time, a few minutes of rocking and singing in his room. He collapses on my chest, his sweet-smelling head under my chin. The stresses and strains of a toddler's life roll off him as his mother holds him close. He has no fretful anxieties. He lets me love and care for him. Sometimes he just rests on me. Sometimes he looks up, and as he meets my eyes a smile breaks out under his thumb. He delights in our relationship, in my loving him, in this time of my holding and cherishing him. It makes me think of the very short, very sweet Psalm 131:

> Oh Lord, my heart is not proud, nor my eyes haughty;
> nor do I involve myself in great matters or things too difficult for me.
> Surely I have composed and quieted my soul;
> Like a leaned child rests against his mother,
> My soul is like a weaned child within me.
> O Israel, hope in the Lord
> From this time forth and forever.
>
> —NASB

I used to read this psalm thinking a *nursing* child might have been a more fitting image than a *weaned* child. A nursing child is visibly very connected with his mother. A weaned child seems more independent. But Josiah has convinced me that the imagery in this psalm is perfect. As a weaned child, he is not coming to me for food. He just wants to be with me. He is relaxed and content because I am with him, not because I am giving him something else that he needs.

Most often what I sing to Josiah in these times is the simple, lovely hymn "Children of the Heavenly Father." This is his special lullaby. I sang it to him during our first days together in Vietnam. I sang it to him (softly!) among strangers and uniformed soldiers as we waited to board the plane out of Ho Chi Minh City. I cherish its image of God the Father tenderly loving and protecting his little Josiah. Sometimes I pray for him while I sing. Sometimes I think about the words of the hymn applied to myself. Sometimes I do not think much at all, but just rest as I sing to my son:

> *Children of the Heavenly Father safely in His bosom gather.*
> *Nestling bird nor star in heaven, such a refuge ever was given.*

What an intimate image, this gathering into our Father's bosom. It seems almost irreverent—how could we be taken into the arms of the omniscient and omnipotent God? What arms? He is Spirit. Yet this is the picture he chooses to give us. "The eternal God is your refuge, and underneath are the everlasting arms" (Dt 33:27). As pictured in Psalm 131 our souls can lean against God. We are children held, somehow, by a strong Father:

> *God His own doth tend and nourish. In His holy courts they flourish.*
> *From all evil things He spares them, in His mighty arms He bears them.*

Here is a tender, nurturing Father creating a home for his children. We want our children to know that home is safe. Because of their backgrounds, it takes time for some adopted children to learn that at home they will be provided for, protected, and loved. At home, with their family, they belong; here they will flourish. God places us in homes. We flourish in "his holy courts," our church homes. We all enter this home in different stages of brokenness, in need of healing and love, and there we learn and grow together with others in our family.

And here again are God's arms protecting us. The line, "from all evil things He spares them" troubles Phil, who points out that God does not always spare his children but sometimes lets them be hurt by evil things. Yes, he sometimes allows what is evil to touch us, but he will not let it destroy us. And ultimately, God will demolish all evil.

Neither life nor death shall ever from the Lord His children sever;
Unto them his grace he showeth, and their sorrows all he knoweth.

Here is a hint that indeed the Lord does not leave us untouched by the evil in the world. God's children know sorrow. But nothing can sever us from him. He chooses to be close to us in our trials and sorrows: "For we do not have a high priest who is unable to sympathize with our weaknesses, but we have one who has been tempted in every way, just as we are—yet was without sin. Let us then approach the throne of grace with confidence, so that we may receive mercy and find grace to help us in our time of need" (Heb 4:16). Jesus understands our sorrows more than anyone. When we suffer, we can look to him. He will draw near to us to give grace and comfort.

Praise the Lord in joyful numbers, your Protector never slumbers;
At the will of your Defender every foeman must surrender.

God our protector and defender always watches us. He is vigilant, and he is stronger than any enemy. We can celebrate this together, "in joyful numbers," and alone: "On my bed I remember you; I think of you through the watches of the night. Because you are my help, I sing in the shadow of your wings" (Ps 63:6–7).

Though He giveth or He taketh, God his children ne'er forsaketh;
His the loving purpose solely to preserve them pure and holy.

As I sing with Josiah I wonder what his future holds. God
has already allowed significant things to be taken from him
before this tender age of eighteen months. The parents who
conceived him and the mother who gave birth to him have
been taken. The orphanage, his first home, has been taken,
along with those who fed and clothed him for his first year of
life. Though God allowed the taking, he was present throughout, not forsaking Josiah but working out his plan to preserve
him pure and holy. For now God has given him a family that
loves him, holds him, and sings to him, and a church body to
nurture him as he grows. Josiah's Father has taken in order to
give. It is comforting to remember that all the givings and
takings of this boy's life are in God's loving hands.

More secure is no one ever than the loved ones of the Savior;
Not yon star on high abiding nor the bird in homenest hiding.

I am glad that Josiah rests in me, but glad also that I am not
the ultimate refuge for him. People ask whether it is frightening to be raising children now, amidst the world's uncertainty
and hatred. We are beset with news of cancer, global warming,
terrorists, and kidnappers. But I need not remove all potential
risks and hazards from my children, nor stay awake all night
to vanquish anything that threatens them. I do what I can, but
their heavenly Father cares for them perfectly. He knows the
number of hairs on their heads, and he calls them more precious than sparrows, whose every move he also watches.

My Josiah is secure, not because of the resources and care
I can muster up for him, but because he is the beloved son of
the heavenly Father. Thus encouraged, I lay my little bird in
his crib of a homenest, where, eyes glazed over, he content-
edly drifts off to sleep.

IN HONOR OF THE BIRTH MOTHERS

Compassion: com-with, pati-to bear, suffer.
Literally, suffering with another;
a sensation of sorrow excited by the distress
or misfortunes of another; pity, commiseration.
—Webster's Revised
Unabridged Dictionary, 1996

Jesus wept.

—John 11:35

God is compassionate. His emotions are not the same as ours, yet in some way (borrowing Webster's words), his sensation of sorrow is excited by the distress of his people.

God does not just tell us about his compassion with general, abstract platitudes. Other religions have instructions to care for needy people. Our holy book shows God himself intervening in the lives of specific people who call out to him including women and including mothers.

Consider the birth mother frightened for her baby son, who leaves him in a basket by the river (Ex 2:1–10), or the wife whose husband and two sons both die, leaving her impoverished and bitter (the book of Ruth). Another woman has a crisis pregnancy after the king commits adultery with her (2 Sm 11). One emotional story tells of a devoted, passionate mother whose only son dies and is brought back to life (2 Kgs 4:8–37). God enters in to each of these women's lives. He protects them and provides for them, sometimes by dramatic miracles, sometimes by sending others to care for them.

We see compassion clearly in the face of Jesus. He is called "a man of sorrows and acquainted with grief" (Is 53:3), and many times we see him enter into the suffering of others. One day Jesus and his disciples were approaching a town and saw a crowd attending the funeral of a young man, the only son of a widow. When Jesus saw the mother, "his heart went out to her and he said, 'Don't cry.'" Then he touched the coffin and told the man to get up. "The dead man sat up and began to talk, and Jesus gave him back to his mother" (Lk 7:11–17). I cherish this image of Jesus moved by the suffering of a mother.

In today's western culture, those who believe that there is a God generally assume that he is compassionate. We are at home with the idea that God cares for individuals in their personal crises, more comfortable with that than with equally biblical ideas of God's judgment and wrath. But those from different cultures do not always know God as compassionate. Many, likely including my sons' birth mothers in Vietnam, only know of gods who may or may not be inclined to help them in their time of need. They perceive God, or gods, as *dis*passionate, removed from their suffering, rather than *com*passionate, suffering with them. What a gift it could be for them to hear about Jesus speaking compassionately to a grieving mother, to know a God who draws near to their sorrow instead of remaining aloof.

When we were waiting for our sons, we prayed for their birth mothers, not knowing anything about them, but trying to imagine their situations. While we were in Vietnam, we were absorbed with the needs of the boys. Now I look back and think again of their birth mothers.

In Vietnam, unmarried women who become pregnant are subject to social disgrace. And married women are encouraged (and sometimes pressured) to have no more than two children. So, both single and married women may stay away from home for several months to hide that they are pregnant.

These pressures, often along with severe poverty, can make it hard to bring a baby into the world. There is another option for pregnant wome that seems easier: About four out of ten pregnancies in Vietnam end in abortion, among the highest percentage of any country in the world. When I read this it takes my breath away. To deliver Benjamin and Josiah into the world was probably agonizing. It probably would have been much easier for two women in Vietnam to have ended these boys' lives than for them to carry them nine months, bear the pain of bringing them into the world, and then go through the anguish of leaving them to be taken by someone else. I gaze at my dear sons, boys made in the image of God, eternal souls with unique personalities and lives full of promise. I cherish the gift of life their birth mothers have given them.

We know more about birth mothers in the United States than about those in Vietnam, partly because of our proximity to them and partly because some have openly shared their stories. We know enough to see that even in our culture there is a wide range of experiences among women who place their children for adoption. Some feel resolution and peace about this difficult chapter of their lives; others have been so ravaged by pain and loss that they feel a need to lobby against adoption. Some birth mothers whose children are in the foster care system want to turn their lives around and bring their children back; others do not. People are complex, and even within our own culture it is hard to make generalizations about birth mothers without misrepresenting some of them. Birth mothers in Vietnam are more hidden from us. Their culture and lives are much different, and they rarely have the opportunity to share their stories.

We know nearly nothing about Benjamin and Josiah's birth mothers, and I do not want to speculate too much about them. I hope to respect their individual dignity by not importing my cultural and personal experience to imagine them into people they may not be. But it is probably safe to assume that these women, the women who first held the boys I call sons, have known great pain. When I think of them, I also experience a little pain—compassion—for them, but I share their suffering only dimly. My sympathy for these women pales next to the compassion of Jesus.

Of all God's acts of compassion perhaps the most stunning occurred while he was dying. "When they came to the place called the Skull, there they crucified him along with the criminals—one on his right, the other on his left. Jesus said, 'Father, forgive them, for they do not know what they are doing'" (Lk 23:34). While reviled and tortured, barely able to speak, Jesus prayed for the forgiveness of his tormentors.

Forgiveness is our great need and God's great work of compassion. When some men lowered their paralyzed friend through a roof in hopes of a healing miracle, everyone was shocked that Jesus's first words were "Your sins are forgiven." After this declaration, he then healed the legs, a confirmation of the greater work of forgiveness. Jesus knew that his promise that day would soon be fulfilled on the cross. In his death, he absorbed our sin and suffering, sealing the benefits of his compassionate forgiveness for all time.

Birth mothers may need many kinds of healing. But, like all of us, what they need most is the compassionate forgiveness of Jesus. When a hurting mother knows the forgiveness of Jesus for herself she will be able to forgive those who have sinned against her. This healing forgiveness can then reach backwards and forwards—back into every time where she has hurt and been hurt, and forward into God's promises of eternal love, which can give her hope even if her current circumstances are harsh. This is the healing that only Jesus can bring, healing made possible by compassion that has suffered.

I look into the faces of my marvelous sons, and I wish that their birth mothers knew how thankful I am to them for carrying and delivering these boys into safekeeping. Even more, I want them to know that God is compassionate. I want them to know that he describes himself as the defender of the widow and orphan, that he sees and cares about their plight. I long for them to have hope and not be hardened by poverty and pain, and I want them to see the face of Jesus and to receive God's comfort. Perhaps they do, through our prayers for them. But perhaps not: "How, then, can they call on the one they have not believed in? And how can they believe in the one of whom they have not heard? And how can they hear without someone preaching to them? And how can they preach unless they are sent? As it is written, 'How beautiful are the feet of those who bring good news!'" (Rom 10:13—15)

How I would rejoice to meet Benjamin and Josiah's birth mothers and learn that someone had loved them in the name of Jesus so that their sorrows were transformed by the compassion of God. How I would rejoice to worship together with them for eternity.

Christians have a history of caring for needy children. Let us also bring good news to their birth mothers. Let us tell them that his heart goes out to them as it did for the widow whose only son died. Let us draw near and listen to someone agonized by the decision of whether to abort a child, or grieving after placing a child for adoption. Let us help her see the tender compassion of God.

SAFETY IN STORMS

I am taught in this ill weather...
to put Him between me and the storm.
—Samuel Rutherford, 1636

The questions came earlier than I expected. Benjamin was still a 3-year-old toddler when he started asking about his beginnings.

Perhaps his sister Clara had something to do with it. One day at breakfast, with all siblings present, she matter-of-factly declared: "Benjamin and Josiah don't know who their real moms are." I was aghast. Where did she ever pick up this "real mom" language? Clara, of all people, for whom Benjamin is closest playmate and most definitely brother, who has never heard us talk about "real moms," who often says that she wishes Benjamin wasn't her brother because then she could marry him. How would this question make Benjamin feel? (Josiah was also a recipient of the declaration but was in happy oblivion, concentrated on the cereal in his bowl.)

"I am their real mom," I quickly told Clara. But I knew that her use of "real mom" simply reflected a lack of vocabulary, so I added: "They just don't know their birth mothers," with a brief explanation.

Did Clara's statement precipitate Benjamin's questions? It's possible, though thoughts had been simmering in his mind. He had been showing interest in his infancy and asked about it often: "When I was a baby, was I cute? When I was a baby, did I go to Grandpa and Grandma's house? When I was a baby, did I sleep in a metal crib?" We answered as best we could: "Yes, you were cute; you did not visit Grandpa and Grandma until you came home when you were almost two; yes, you slept in a metal crib." He wanted to look at the pictures of the orphanage and our trip to adopt him. We tried to stay alert to what might be going on in his inner life.

When we drive by the local hospital, Kathryn and Clara enjoy pointing out where they were born. On one of those drives, shortly after the "real mom" breakfast, Benjamin asked where he was born. I thought quickly about how to answer, wondering if I should go beyond the basic: "We don't know exactly where you were born," or "You were born in Vietnam and stayed in the orphanage until we brought you home." I ventured one of those simple answers. I then asked another question to explore whether it was bothering Benjamin that he was not born in the same hospital as his sisters. But his attention was taken with a passing motorcycle and he lost interest.

A few weeks later I was again driving with the four children when Benjamin's voice came up from the rear of the van: "Mama, whose tummy did I come out of?" I prayed quickly for wisdom to answer. I knew these questions would come but wasn't expecting them now, from the rear of the van, with all other siblings listening in. I answered Benjamin generally again, assuring him that though we did not know who gave him birth, I was his mother and would be for the rest of his life.

Adoptive parents can be troubled by these kinds of questions. We want to be honest but not give our children information they are not ready to absorb. We want to speak just the right words to soothe any unsettledness they may be feeling, and we want to answer their questions while also protecting their emotional security.

In the same season as these interactions with Benjamin, I woke up one night to the sounds of a storm. Wind and rain pummeled the house, shrieking and battering. It sounded bit-

terly cold. I was glad to be snuggled under a warm blanket in
a well heated home. As I lay awake, sheltered from the wailing
tumult outside, I thought about Benjamin's questions and my
own. Are these questions the beginning of an identity crisis?
What kind of anxiety will our boys' adoptions bring them?
How will it surface? Will they grieve because of their past?
How can I best shepherd and love them through these questions and anything that worries them later?

It is comforting to lie safe in a warm, dark room while a
storm rages outside. The blankets feel especially cozy; so does
the presence of loved ones safe under the roof together. My
thoughts drift from storms to adoption and back. My sons
may someday be assailed by other kinds of storms, tempests
of doubts and grief. Questions may batter against them. But
we can bear those storms if we encounter them while safe in
a strong shelter. I can listen to the questions as I listen to the
wind this night, knowing that what sounds menacing does
not have the power to harm. We can endure a fearsome storm
if our shelter is strong.

Adoptive families of the past, encouraged by their social
workers, tried to keep out the storms by concealing their
children's backgrounds. Babies were sometimes smuggled to
parents at night so others would not know they were adopted.
Children might not be told of their adoptions until they were
teenagers or adults, and sometimes not at all. It was thought
best to give adopted children a blank slate on which to begin
their new life. But families and counselors found that trying
to bury the past was not foolproof—some adoptees still felt
battered by insecurity and grief. Denying the storms might
have increased their devastation when they did strike.

Now adoption professionals encourage us to talk about
our child's past often and in as much detail as possible. The
assumption is that there will be menacing storms, and we are
encouraged to tell our children to let them come, maybe even

to stand out in them. Some suggest that we ask leading questions to explore things that may be troubling our children, that we tell them in advance that they may sometimes feel confused or angry or sad.

But each child, teenager, and adult is unique. Some are settled in their identity and feel no battering from unresolved questions. Some experience a passing shower, mild curiosity that is easily resolved. Others are slammed hard with frightening questions and doubts. If we insist that our children will have pain and identity confusion, when some of them really may not, might that not also increase the potential power of the storms in their lives?

What if we focus not on the storm, but on the refuge? As I lie in bed, I am thankful for my walls and roof. As we shepherd our children, we can draw them with us into places protected by the walls and roof of God. He calls himself refuge, stronghold, shield, fortress, and tower—each of which suggests the same comforting shelter as a warm house during a night of storm. "I love you, O Lord, my strength. The Lord is my rock, my fortress and my deliverer; my God is my rock, in whom I take refuge. He is my shield and the horn of my salvation, my stronghold" (Ps 18:1–2). We can hide in God. We can enjoy his presence as he shelters us through the storms of our lives.

The young widow Ruth was vulnerable and helpless, unemployed and poor. There was no evidence of a secure future for her, but Boaz recognized that she had found a place of safety: "May you be richly rewarded by the Lord, the God of Israel, under whose wings you have come to take refuge" (Ru 2:10). Ruth's great-grandson David spent years living as a fugitive, hiding first from a king who wanted to murder him and years later from his own treacherous son, Absalom. Like his great-grandmother Ruth, he cherished the protection of God: "On my bed I remember you; I think of you through the watches of the night. Because you are my help, I sing in the shadow of your wings. My soul clings to you; your right hand upholds me" (Ps 63:6–7). I have inherited this legacy as I lay awake at night relishing my refuge.

I hope to be like Ruth in sharing the security of this stronghold with my children and grandchildren: "He who fears the Lord has a secure fortress, and for his children it will be a refuge" (Prv 14:26). What a wonderful verse for adoptive parents! Right now, my faith in the Lord is the refuge for my children. They are safe in upheaval because of my relationship with God. We do not need to deny or ignore the storms, nor do we need to stand outside and expect them to harm us. These children share a home with us, their parents. We share a physical shelter and we share a refuge of faith. Together we listen to the storms, if they come, while together abiding in the stronghold of God. We do not need to try to conceal the storms. We can acknowledge them. But we experience the threats of wind and thunder together from a safe place.

Later, we hope the refuge of faith that shields our children will be their own, built by years of listening to the words of Jesus and putting them into practice. We hope our children will know that God's protection is stronger than any storm that might frighten them. Perilous tempests will prove the strength of the refuge and make it even more cherished by those safe inside.

I need not fear storms that may threaten my children. I need not have all the right answers in fearful times. I only need to be with them in the fortress, to put God between them and the storm. That God is my refuge *is* the answer for my children.

LITANY OF THANKS

You are my God, and I will give you thanks;
you are my God, and I will exalt you.
Give thanks to the Lord, for he is good;
his love endures forever.
—Psalm 118:28–29

I give thanks for Benjamin and Josiah, dear boys knit together by God. Each of them is a wonder.

> *Give thanks to the Lord, for he is good.*
> *His faithfulness continues to all generations.*

I give thanks for their birth mothers. I look at Benjamin and Josiah and am unspeakably thankful that those two women chose to bring them into the world instead of ending their lives in the womb.

> *Give thanks to the Lord, for he is good.*
> *His faithfulness continues to all generations.*

I give thanks for Benjamin and Josiah's unique life adventures. A story gets passed around adoption circles about a father who says that he knows that some of his children are adopted, but can't remember which. I appreciate the intent of the story in stressing that adopted children are as much a part of a family as birth children, but I am glad to remember my children's adoptions and will speak of them gratefully. God brought them into the world and into our family in special ways that are their heritage and part of his eternal plan for them.

Give thanks to the Lord, for he is good.
His faithfulness continues to all generations.

I give thanks for the privilege of being a mother. It is an honor to love my children and influence them for eternity. I am thankful for how God is molding me through them.

Give thanks to the Lord, for he is good.
His faithfulness continues to all generations.

I give thanks for the relationships among my four children. God took two girls from my body and two boys from the other side of the world and forged them together for a lifetime of relationship. I rejoice when Josiah puts out his arms trustingly to "Da-da," his name for big sister Kathryn, and when Benjamin and Clara romp and explore and laugh together. I am thankful for the joy they have in each other now and for the hope of relationships that will, Lord willing, be precious to them for the rest of their lives and into eternity.

Give thanks to the Lord, for he is good.
His faithfulness continues to all generations.

I give thanks for how my sons have heightened some of the joys of daily life. Shortly after Benjamin's homecoming, a friend overheard him call me "Mama" and remarked that it was beautiful. We take for granted most instances of a two-year-old calling for his mother; that this two-year-old calls me by name is exciting and cherished.

I read a book with Josiah that includes a picture of a penguin family; he points to them: "Mama, Papa, Baby." He has concluded that a group of big and little penguins (or people) standing together must be a family. I probably would not have reveled in this interpretation with my daughters, but with Josiah I rejoice—before the age of sixteen months he had no concept of a family; by the time he is two, family is so integral to his life that he sees other families all over.

The boys' first prayers and songs to Jesus are especially sweet. Because they were not introduced to the Lord from birth we cherish the privilege of watching them come to know and worship him.

> *Give thanks to the Lord, for he is good.*
> *His faithfulness continues to all generations.*

I am thankful for the trials and tears of the adoptions and for tumult that may still come. They reveal my poverty of faith, leading me limping into the arms of my heavenly Father. God gives special treasures in times of weakness and pain. I would not bypass those difficult times if I were given the choice now, because of the riches that have come with them.

> *Give thanks to the Lord, for he is good.*
> *His faithfulness continues to all generations.*

I am thankful for my life in the church, for how he loves my children and me through others. I am thankful for how the adoptions revealed to me the interconnectedness of God's people. I am thankful to have companions on my pilgrimage through life.

Give thanks to the Lord, for he is good.
His faithfulness continues to all generations.

I am thankful for God's word, thankful that he uses human language to communicate with us. These words have sustained men and women and children for thousands of years, and they have sustained me. I am thankful for how God has used his word to feed me. I am thankful that in it he has given us everything we need to follow him.

Give thanks to the Lord, for he is good.
His faithfulness continues to all generations.

I am thankful that when we venture out in faith to follow Jesus he does more than we could ask or imagine. I am thankful that he touches our weak work with Christ's power and that through it he is glorified throughout all generations (Eph 3:20–21).

Give thanks to Lord, for he is good.
His faithfulness continues to all generations.

I am thankful for his redemptive work that has made it all possible.

HOSANNA

It is Palm Sunday. It is also three days after Josiah's home-coming and sixteen months after newly arrived Benjamin intently watched us singing "Angels We Have Heard on High" around the table.

At breakfast we again break out into spontaneous singing. Our children delight in the "Hosanna" choruses that are filled with the exuberance of exalting in Jesus as King. Kathryn and Clara start singing from their seats: "Hosanna, Hosanna, Hosanna in the Highest" while Josiah, in my arms by the sink, watches with great interest. I start moving with him to the rhythm of the song; we dance a bit. One of his first smiles at home shyly emerges, to everyone's great delight. Thus encouraged, up from chairs the others bounce, dancing and singing. The kitchen becomes a happy melee of moving arms and legs.

Josiah is now smiling completely. His family is new to him, yet he can enjoy our presence and happiness, and somehow start to enter into our praise of the Lord. He is beginning to know the joy of worshipping God.

I witness with deep thankfulness as my son is enfolded into the worship of Jesus Christ. He is ready to receive a family's love, and to begin to know and love his Maker. We have the privilege of touching on a pump that has been primed until water is at the edge, ready to gush out.

Singing "Angels We Have Heard on High," we looked back to the glorious time when the God of the Universe entered our world on his mission to redeem us and we join in the praise of the angels who announced his arrival. Singing "Hosanna," we look back to the time when his quest was reaching its climax and we sing with the children who ran along the road with him.

In *glorias* and *hosanna*s, we also look forward to the time when God's redemptive quest will be finally and completely fulfilled and we will sing praise where there are no more tears. Kathryn, Clara, Benjamin, and Josiah, we pray, will be swept up together with us and with all of God's adopted children. We will be united with all of his people and we will sing in loud chorus as we are carried safely home. This morning is a blessed foretaste. We will be worshipping together, forever.

Hosanna.

APPENDIX 1

LIGHT FOR THE JOURNEY
SCRIPTURE TO ENCOURAGE AND CHALLENGE

The following are a few of the words that have sustained me on my adoption journeys. May they give you security when you are afraid, hope when you are hopeless, and help when you do not know how to pray. May they lead you into other parts of the Bible and draw you near to God. May they ignite your wonder and faith and strengthen you to keep pressing on.

God's Adoption of His Children

He came to that which was his own, but his own did not receive him. Yet to all who received him, to those who believed in his name, he gave the right to become children of God—children born not of natural descent, nor of human decision or a husband's will, but born of God.

John 1:11–13

For you did not receive a spirit that makes you a slave again to fear, but you received the Spirit of sonship. And by him we cry, "Abba, Father." The Spirit himself testifies with our spirit that we are God's children.

Romans 8:15–16

But when the time had fully come, God sent his Son, born of a woman, born under law, to redeem those under law, that we might receive the full rights of sons. Because you are sons, God sent the Spirit of his Son into our hearts, the Spirit who calls out, "Abba, Father." So you are no longer a slave, but a son; and since you are a son, God has made you also an heir.

Galatians 4:4–7

For he chose us in him before the creation of the world to be holy and blameless in his sight. In love he predestined us to be adopted as his sons through Jesus Christ, in accordance with his pleasure and will—to the praise of his glorious grace, which he has freely given us in the One he loves.

Ephesians 1:4–6

How great is the love the Father has lavished on us, that we should be called children of God! And that is what we are! The reason the world does not know us is that it did not know him. Dear friends, now we are children of God, and what we will be has not yet been made known. But we know that when he appears, we shall be like him, for we shall see him as he is.

1 John 3:1-2

God's Care for Orphans

He defends the cause of the fatherless and the widow, and loves the alien, giving him food and clothing.

Deuteronomy 10:18

He raises the poor from the dust and lifts the needy from the ash heap; he seats them with princes and has them inherit a throne of honor.

1 Samuel 2:8

"Because of the oppression of the weak and the groaning of the needy, I will now arise," says the Lord. "I will protect them from those who malign them."

Psalm 12:5

A father to the fatherless, a defender of widows, is God in his holy dwelling.

Psalm 68:5

He upholds the cause of the oppressed and gives food to the hungry. The Lord sets prisoners free, the Lord gives sight to the blind, the Lord lifts up those who are bowed down, the Lord loves the righteous. The Lord watches over the alien and sustains the fatherless and the widow, but he frustrates the ways of the wicked.

Psalm 146:7–9

Arise, Lord! Lift up your hand, O God. Do not forget the helpless. Why does the wicked man revile God? Why does he say to himself, "He won't call me to account"? But you, O God, do see trouble and grief; you consider it to take it in hand. The victim commits himself to you; you are the helper of the fatherless. Break the arm of the wicked and evil man; call him to account for his wickedness that would not be found out. The Lord is King for ever and ever; the nations will perish from his land. You hear, O Lord, the desire of the afflicted; you encourage them, and you listen to their cry, defending the fatherless and the oppressed, in order that man, who is of the earth, may terrify no more.

Psalm 10:12–18

The Spirit of the Sovereign Lord is on me, because the Lord has anointed me to preach good news to the poor. He has sent me to bind up the brokenhearted, to proclaim freedom for the captives and release from darkness for the prisoners, to proclaim the year of the Lord's favor and the day of vengeance of our God, to comfort all who mourn, and provide for those who grieve in Zion- to bestow on them a crown of beauty instead of ashes, the oil of gladness instead of mourning, and a garment of praise instead of a spirit of despair. They will be called oaks of righteousness, a planting of the Lord for the display of his splendor.

Isaiah 61:1–3

Our Responsibility for Orphans

Do not take advantage of a widow or an orphan. If you do and they cry out to me, I will certainly hear their cry. My anger will be aroused, and I will kill you with the sword; your wives will become widows and your children fatherless.

Exodus 22:22–24

Defend the cause of the weak and fatherless; maintain the rights of the poor and oppressed. Rescue the weak and needy; deliver them from the hand of the wicked.

Psalm 82:3–4

Learn to do right! Seek justice, encourage the oppressed. Defend the cause of the fatherless, plead the case of the widow.

Isaiah 1:17

Religion that God our Father accepts as pure and faultless is this: to look after orphans and widows in their distress and to keep oneself from being polluted by the world.

James 1:27

Dear friends, since God so loved us, we also ought to love one another. No one has ever seen God; but if we love one another, God lives in us and his love is made complete in us.

1 John 4:11–12

Promises and Exhortations for
Adopted Children and Their Parents

I am still confident of this: I will see the goodness of the Lord in the land of the living. Wait for the Lord; be strong and take heart and wait for the Lord.

Psalm 27:13–14

I waited patiently for the Lord; he turned to me and heard my cry. He lifted me out of the slimy pit, out of the mud and mire; he set my feet on a rock and gave me a firm place to stand.

Psalm 40:1–2

Even in darkness light dawns for the upright, for the gracious and compassionate and righteous man.

Psalm 112:4

The Lord watches over you- the Lord is your shade at your right hand; the sun will not harm you by day, nor the moon by night. The Lord will keep you from all harm- he will watch over your life; the Lord will watch over your coming and going both now and forevermore.

Psalm 121:5–8

Those who sow in tears will reap with songs of joy. He who goes out weeping, carrying seed to sow, will return with songs of joy, carrying sheaves with him.

Psalm 126:5–6

For you created my inmost being; you knit me together in my mother's womb. I praise you because I am fearfully and wonderfully made; your works are wonderful, I know that full well. My frame was not hidden from you when I was made in the secret place. When I was woven together in the depths of the earth, your eyes saw my unformed body. All the days ordained for me were written in your book before one of them came to be.

Psalm 139:13–16

He who fears the Lord has a secure fortress, and for his children it will be a refuge.

Proverbs 14:26

Can a mother forget the baby at her breast and have no compassion on the child she has borne? Though she may forget, I will not forget you! See, I have engraved you on the palms of my hands; your walls are ever before me. Your sons hasten back, and those who laid you waste depart from you.

Isaiah 49:15-17

"Which of you, if his son asks for bread, will give him a stone? Or if he asks for a fish, will give him a snake? If you, then, though you are evil, know how to give good gifts to your children, how much more will your Father in heaven give good gifts to those who ask him!

Matthew 7:9–11

So do not worry, saying, 'What shall we eat?' or 'What shall we drink?' or 'What shall we wear?' For the pagans run after all these things, and your heavenly Father knows that you need them.

Matthew 6:31–32

Be joyful in hope, patient in affliction, faithful in prayer.

Romans 12:12

Therefore he is able to save completely those who come to God through him, because he always lives to intercede for them.

Hebrews 7:25

You are my God, and I will give you thanks;
you are my God, and I will exalt you.
Give thanks to the Lord, for he is good;
his love endures forever.

Psalm 118:28–29

APPENDIX 2

ADOPTION RESOURCES

Websites on adoption abound. The internet has become the preferred means for many adoptive families to acquire information and communicate with each other. This plethora of adoption web sites can be a source for good information and encouragement—and also potentially for information overload and confusion. I have limited this list to an adoption/orphan care agency, an adoption resource center tied in with a larger Christian ministry, and several web-based clearinghouses of adoption articles and information. All sites include links to more information.

HOPE'S PROMISE

www.hopespromise.com
Phone 303-660-0277

The adoption agency that brought our boys home! *Hope's Promise* facilitates domestic and international adoptions, and also serves children through their Orphan Ministries program. From their webpage: "The values underlying the conception and ongoing existence of Hope's Promise include an evangelical Christian world view in which every individual is recognized as created in the image of God, worthy of respect, and in need of a right relationship with their God. Children are esteemed; and families are believed to be God's institution of choice for developing healthy individuals." Website includes a resource center with recommended books and links to other sites. (Note: We worked with Hope's Promise, a Colorado-based adoption agency, while living in Michigan. Adopting through an out-of-state agency is possible but involves some extra paperwork.)

HOPE FOR ORPHANS

www.familylife.com/hopefororphans
Phone 1-800-358-6329

Hope for Orphans is a ministry of FamilyLife Services, started "to support God's work to bring orphans to Christian families and to Himself." It seeks to help the American church care for orphans, especially through adoption. They offer "If You Were Mine" workshops for families considering adoption; their website also contains information about adoption and links to other adoption-related sites.

GENERAL ADOPTION INFORMATION

The following sites contain information about many aspects of adoption, as well as discussion groups, books, and links to adoption agencies and other resources:

Joint Council on International Children's Services:

www.jcics.org

National Council for Adoption: www.ncfa-usa.org
National Adoption Information Clearinghouse:

www.naic.acf.hhs.gov

www.adoption.com

End notes

Preface
[1]John Piper, Sermon 6/20/04, © Desiring God.
Website: www.desiringGod.org.

Introduction
[2]John Piper, *God's Passion for His Glory,* Crossway Books,
1998, p. 29.

Adoption as Worship
[3]Ron Sider, *Rich Christians in an Age of Hunger,* 2nd edition,
Downer's Grove, IL, InterVarsity Press, 1984, p. 173.

[4]Marianne Takas and Edward Warner, *To Love a Child,*
Addison-Wesley, 1992, p.141.

[5]Lee Varon, *Adopting on Your Own,* New York, Farrar, Straus
and Giroux, 2000, p. 7–8.

Vulnerabilities Awakened
[6]Adam Perlman, *Adoption Nation,* New York, Basic Books,
2000, pp. 12, 18, 29.

Born of God
[7]Karin Evans, *The Lost Daughters of China,* New York,
Tarcher/Putnam, 2000, p. 141.

[8]J.I. Packer, *Knowing God,* Downer's Grove, IL,
InterVarsity Press, 1973, p. 199.

A Mother's Heart
[9]John Stott, *Romans,* Downer's Grove, IL,
InterVarsity Press, 1994, p.142-143.

He is Good
[10]C.S. Lewis, *The Lion, the Witch, and the Wardrobe*, New York, MacMillan, 1951, p. 64.

Birthday Gifts
[11]John Piper, Sermon, June 20, 2004, www.desiringGod.org.

Facets of Prayer
[12]Sinclair Ferguson, *The Christian Life: A Doctrinal Introduction*, Carlisle, PA: The Banner of Truth Trust, 1981, p. 94.

Orphans and Widows
[13]John Ensor, *Answering the Call*, Focus on the Family, p. 102.

[14]George Grant, *Third Time Around: A History of the Pro-Life Movement from the First Century to the Present,* Wolgemuth & Hyatt, 1991, p. 12.

Safely Home
[15]J.I. Packer, *Knowing God,* p.184.

[16]J.I. Packer, *Knowing God,* p. 203.

Incarnation
[17]Dr. and Mrs. Howard Taylor, *Hudson Taylor and the China Inland Mission: The Growth of a Work of God,* OMF International, Singapore, 1911 (reprint 1998).

In Honor of the the Orphans
[18]Elizabeth Sloglund, *Amma: The Life and Words of Amy Carmichael*, Grand Rapids, Baker Books, 1999, p. 32.

[19]FamilyLife, *If you Were Mine*, Little Rock, Arkansas, 2004, p. 8.

[20]Laura Bobak, "For Sale: The Innocence of Cambodia," *Ottawa (Ontario) Sun*, October 24, 1996; "UNICEF Hails Entry Into Force of Optional Protocol on the Sale of Children, Child Prostitution and Child Pornography," New York, October 23, 2001, http:www.unicef.org/newsline/01pr81.htm (accessed June 2005).

[21]Laura Bobak, "The Deadly Streets of Guatemala," *Ottawa (Ontario) Sun*, October 21, 1996.

[22]Laura Bobak, "Rwanda's Orphans of War," *Ottawa (Ontario) Sun*, October 22, 1996; "Africa's Orphan Crisis: Worst is Yet to Com," Johannesburg/Geneva, November 26, 2003, http:www.unicef.org/media/media_16287.html (accessed June 2005).

[23]Personal correspondence with the author, June 2005; foster care statistics from *If you were Mine*, p. 8.

ABOUT THE AUTHOR

After graduating from the University of Michigan, Kristin Wong lived with her husband Phil in San Diego, California, and later moved to Shanghai, China, where they spent a year teaching English to college students and teachers. Now back in Michigan, she finds her life very full serving a growing family and growing church. She has written curriculum for children and helps lead and teach her church's fellowship for mothers. She is enriched by her university community and has been privileged to host college students and missionaries from Central Asia, China, India, Italy, Haiti, Romania, Slovakia, and Thailand.

In moments of free time, Kristin enjoys her cello, conversation with friends, early morning walks, days by the lake, and traveling. When she can't explore new places herself, she finds that homeschooling allows her some vicarious travel—she loves reading great books with her children.

Kristin revels in speaking about the beauty and riches of adoption. This is her first book.